"*The Suitcase* is a creative teen novel that will keep you reading to find out what happens as the storyline of a young teen girl with all her relationship troubles and issues unfolds. Each relationship is vital in life: Father/daughter, mother/daughter, friendships and ultimately the relationship with Jesus Christ. All are addressed and played out with all the pain felt and the victories enjoyed. This is recommended reading for teens and parents alike."
                    —Chad McComas, Editor of *The Christian Journal*

The Suitcase

Priscilla Tate Gilmore

ISBN 978-1-0980-8436-3 (paperback)
ISBN 978-1-0980-8437-0 (digital)

Christian Faith Publishing
832 Park Avenue
Meadville, PA 16335
www.christianfaithpublishing.com

This is a fictional story based on true events. The places referred to in this novel are real.

Printed in the United States of America

To Matthew and Sarah, you are priceless treasures. I love you.

Let us run with perseverance the race marked out for us. Let us fix our eyes on Jesus, the author and perfector of our faith.

—Hebrews 12:2

The rain came down, the streams rose, and the winds blew and beat against that house; yet it did not fall because it had its foundation on the rock.

— Matthew 7:25

Chapter 1

hill from the snow reaches through my down-lined jacket and bites my bones. I watch Daddy walk farther and farther away. I cup my shivering hands around my mouth and yell, "Daddy, come back." Then I wake and realize I was reliving a bad but true to life dream.

My dream is believable because Daddy really did leave a decade ago. One minute he was in the house and the next, he was gone—forever.

Today, I'm so tired, tired from staying up late thinking about Daddy that I don't want to go to school. Needing a few more zzzs, I snuggle down in my bed. The soft light blue down comforter wraps around me like a butterfly in a cocoon.

Mom's voice echoes from the other side of my bedroom door. "Beth, can I come in?"

"No. Go away."

The door latch releases.

Annoyed, I roll over onto my back. Mom stands next to my bed ready for work. She's dressed in gray pants, a cream crochet-laced shell, and her favorite electric pink blazer. And, as always, her flawless pink fingernails.

"It's almost seven," she says. "Your breakfast is getting—"

I unwrap myself, sit up, and interrupt. "Yikes. I stayed up remembering Daddy and forgot to set the alarm. Mom, do you recall that Daddy left ten years ago yesterday?"

Mom glances around. A tear balances on her eyelashes, but she brushes it away with her palm and swallows hard. "Your room looks like a tornado blew through. Why haven't you cleaned up the piles of shirts, pants, and shoes? Beth Paine, do it today after school." Mom walks toward the door.

I fold my arms and call to her back. "Mom, you're more concerned about my collection of stuff instead of talking to me and meeting my pain. Why won't you tell me what happened ten years ago? When I was little, we had 'Mommy and Me Times.' We talked about everything. Mom, even though I'm older now, I still need time for heart-to-heart discussions. I'm ready to hear what you need to tell me. Did I do something wrong to make Daddy leave? How am I supposed to become emotionally stable if you won't talk? Mom, write a note to excuse me from classes. I'll miss school for the day so you can tell me about the unknown that is destroying my life."

With her hand on the door, Mom spins halfway around and faces me. "Get rid of your anger, Beth." Then she eyeballs the piles again, shakes her head, and leaves. The door closes with a click.

I run across the room, open the door, and yell after Mom. "I'm not angry, just confused." I slam the door, lean against it, and rip off a splintered fingernail. My focus boomerangs to the photo of Daddy on the nightstand. I think aloud, "Where did you go? Why didn't you come home? Every time I think about you, I remember the smell of your Aqua Velva aftershave, and I cry harder and longer, missing you so much."

Over the years, I've come to suspect that Daddy either died suddenly or that he and Mom divorced. Either way, I got no closure at age six. No goodbyes. And no final hugs from the man who was so important to me. Daddy never said, "I'll come back, Beth."

Wishing I could understand and get closure, I inhale, blow out the breath, and appoint myself as "Female Agent 007." I vow to keep asking questions and do anything I need to do to get answers and find out why Daddy left. With nose dripping, I run to the bathroom to grab Kleenex and a quick shower.

After showering, I reach for a towel. My toenail catches on a sharp corner of the molding. I scream, "Ouch!" Blood oozes from the gash and makes a small puddle on the white tile. Am I supposed to suffer forever? I apply a bandage, dress, and fly down the stairs to the kitchen.

Mom sits at the kitchen table, talking quietly to RC (short for Robert Cade Jr.). A year after Daddy left, Mom's last name changed from Paine to Cade when she married Robert. They had Stephanie

(Steph for short), who's cute and smart for an eight-year-old and RC, who is a quiet five-year-old.

Mom notices me in the doorway and looks up with a smile cemented on her face. *Did she forget about our face off?*

"Beth, I reheated your breakfast in the microwave," Mom says. Then she lifts the yellow smiley face coffee mug off the oak table and presses it against her red lips. Then she swallows what I suspect is her usual expresso with a dash of cream and sugar and sets the mug back on the table.

A moment of silence follows. I decide to move on because I'm in no mood to stick around. I walk over to the table and place my hands on the back of my chair and look at my breakfast, which is a twice-cooked, egg-filled burrito. My lip curls. "Mom, after track practice last night, Coach Forsythe reminded all of us about the meeting before school today. If I don't run now, I'll be super late." I choose to not tell her that the garbage disposal will love the meal.

"You haven't eaten."

"I'll get something from McDonald's on my way. I love you, Mom." I kiss her on the cheek, turn, and zip like the Road Runner to the hall. Then I grab my backpack with a photo of Daddy tucked in the pocket and bolt out the door to my blue Chevy Cruze.

❋ ❋ ❋

Minutes later, I park in the student lot of Glendale High. Still annoyed with Mom for not talking, I squeeze the wrappings of my McDonald's Egg McMuffin into a tight ball and toss the garbage in a litterbag on the floorboard. Then I hoist my backpack over my shoulder, slide on my sunglasses, and look for Molly.

My longtime friend Molly walks alone toward the gym. In elementary school, Molly and I were inseparable. We had sleepovers, sat next to each other, and linked arms everywhere we went. People thought Molly was my twin. Our motto was "Friends Forever." But last year, she discovered a new friend—Josh. I mean boys are great and all, but why can't Molly and I still be close. The only thing that Molly and I do together, aside from running with the track team, is an occasional shopping spree. Lately, she's been downright nasty, and I don't know why. I keep trying to put the friendship back together again.

Hoping she will listen to my heartache, I rush to catch up. "Hey, Molly."

Molly halts and flashes a grin. "Like my new clothes, Beth?" Dressed in whitewash skinny-leg jeans, sleek red floral print tunic, and white lace-up platform boots, Molly exhibits an arrogant confidence by performing a pirouette.

"Sure."

"Hope Josh like them." Then, looking everywhere but at me, Molly squints in the sunlight. "He should be here soon."

After her statement, I guesstimate that this is going to be one of Molly's no-time-for-small-talk moments. I adjust my sunglasses. "I don't think I did very well on the English test yesterday."

Molly shifts books from one arm to the other and looks straight at me. "Why?"

I search her eyes for understanding. "Don't think I did well on the test because I was missing my dad. It's been ten years."

Molly drums her fingers on her notebook, shifts her weight restlessly, and fiddles with her hair. "Stop whining, Beth. Be glad you have Robert for a stepfather." Her eyes dart like missiles from side to side, apparently still searching for Josh.

My eyes narrow. I spit angry words. "Molly, why do you want me to shut up about my problem? Maybe if you talked about your troubles. It would bring us closer. I'm willing to listen."

"I don't have problems. I'm doing just fine."

Even though the words sound like snakelike hisses, Molly's black licorice eyelashes bat faster than wings on a hummingbird. I suspect she's blinking back tears. Without skipping a beat, Molly adds, "Beth, get on with your life."

Silence stands between us. My thoughts race. *Is she jealous? Is she hurting? Why won't Molly tell all like someone I know? Me.*

Molly tucks a windblown lock of hair behind her ear, turns on her heel, and trots off. I stand, paralyzed, watching Molly.

Josh rounds the flagpole and jogs toward Molly. The two meet. Molly locks her hands around his neck. Josh wraps his arms around her waist. The twosome locks lips for what seems like forever. Then they walk hand in hand toward the gym.

I resist the urge to run up, grab, and kick her for treating me like I was an irritating gnat. I march with heavy steps toward the track meeting and find a seat on the gym's bleachers just as Coach Forsythe calls the assembly to order.

"Okay, quiet down," Coach says. "Practice will continue every day Monday through Friday after school. Practices will be tough. Our first out-of-town track meet will be one week from this coming Saturday, March 23 at Trabuco Hills High in Mission Viejo. Then meets will happen every two weeks until the end of the season. I'm counting on each of you to qualify for state championships."

The track team not only includes Molly, Josh, and me, but Jimmy, Susan, and Brian. Our team is called "Squad of Six." In addition to running, we eat lunch together and occasionally just hang out.

Twelve minutes before first period, the coach dismisses us with, "I'll see you after school on the track at three thirty sharp."

I slip out of the gym and make my way toward geometry. Jimmy flags me down and yells, "Beth, wait up."

Jimmy approaches. Every time I see him, my pulse quickens at his broad warm grin and the twinkle from his blueberry-colored eyes. Jimmy brings his handsome lean six-foot body to a gentle stop in front of me. "Beth, want to come over after track practice tomorrow, work on the '57 Chevy, and stay for dinner?"

"Sure. What are we going to work on now?"

"Same thing as last week—sanding. Then after sanding, we'll spray on another coat of primer. My dad will tell us when the car doesn't look like rippling water. I know you don't like getting sprayed with orange sandpaper dust, but I like having you around."

"I like our times in your garage too, Jimmy."

A smile jumps from Jimmy to me and then springs back to him. Then he says, "Gotta go. See you at lunch."

I walk toward the Geometry 1 classroom, not thinking about points, lines and planes, logic and reasoning, angles, slopes, triangles, polygons, circles or any other mathematical terms. I open the classroom door.

The teacher, Mr. Max, meets me at the entrance and asks loudly in his monotone voice, "Beth, are you going to sign up for the SAT? The last day to register is Friday, May 5."

Why is he so anxious? It's only March. Why did he single me out in front of the whole class? Was it because I was the last one in? Wish Max would stop fretting over me and quit trying to force me to do what others are doing just because it's the norm. Will the test show me what to do with my life and guarantee happiness? Don't think so. I remember reading a poem about a traveler who reached a fork in the road and was forced to make a decision. I'm trying to convince myself and others that it's okay to take the road less traveled and be different. Honestly, I haven't given any thought to the SAT because right now, all I want to do is get through high school.

Thirty pairs of eyes gawk at me. Feeling the heat from my suspected red face, I search my brain for words. I come up with the idea that maybe a little white lie will get Mr. Max off my back. I answer, "Thinking on it." Sweat forms on my upper lip.

Mr. Max raises his eyebrows and runs fingers through wisps of thinning gray hair. Then he tells the class, "Turn to page 175 in your books."

I rush to my seat, wishing this class wasn't a college requirement. I bend an elbow on my desk, rest my head on the knuckles, read the page, and watch the clock's second hand erase the hour—slowly.

Thankfully, the hour passes without any further interrogations from Mr. Max. I slip into the hallway congested with students. My worry is that Miss King, my English Lit teacher, will grill me about my test score. After what just happened, I don't need or want any more pressure or questions.

Miss King turns my way as I cross the threshold. "Beth, I need to speak with you after class." She broadcasts the announcement like a reporter for the evening news. Lucky me. Is there a large sign posted on campus somewhere that reads, "Teachers, Kick Beth While She's

Down"? Has this day been declared for the sole purpose of embarrassing me?

Miss King turns and faces those seated. "Class, I've graded your tests from yesterday's exam. You can pick them up before you leave."

I plant my body on a chair in front of Molly and throw the backpack under the desk. Molly taps me on the shoulder and says loudly in my ear, "Yep, you failed."

With half an ear, I listen to Miss King read a poem by Edgar Allan Poe. I sigh. Because poetry is my least favorite in the literary world, my thoughts wander until I'm brought back to the classroom after hearing notebooks snap. Miss King reminds everyone as they stand to leave. "Don't forget your papers. See you tomorrow."

Molly gathers girls in the back of the room and they giggle-snicker-point-whisper.

I scowl at Molly and her group. Then I gather my books and shuffle toward the front. "You wanted to see me, Miss King?"

Miss King sits on the edge of her oversize gray metal desk, somersaulting a pencil in her left hand. She looks over the black-rimmed reading glasses that rest on the tip of her nose and hands me my test with a large red "F" circled at the top of the paper. "Beth, what happened? Did you not understand something? It's not like you. Are you okay?"

Words catch in my throat. "Family problems." It's not a lie. I tilt my head and glare. "Won't happen again. May I go now?"

"Okay, Beth," Miss King says. Then she rests her head on an open palm and sighs. "See you tomorrow."

Tears cloud my eyes. Pain swells in my chest. Embarrassed for the second time, I turn, march out of the room, slam the door behind me, and run to my car. Before starting the engine and heading home, I collapse onto the warm gray upholstery. Tears rush down my cheeks like water over Yosemite Falls.

Chapter 2

I arrive home, emotionally spent. All I want to do is go to my room and do nothing, nothing that requires brain power. With a firm grip on the front door handle, I push the door open and slip in. A soft click follows as it latches.

Mom's voice comes from the kitchen, "Beth, is that you?"

My shoulders slump. "Ugh." I drop my backpack, and it lands with the sound of a small thunderclap.

"Come see what I've got."

I turn and stare at my reflection in the hall mirror. Then I cover my puffy red eyes with my sunglasses and suck in air and round the corner.

I see Mom and Mrs. Cummings seated at the kitchen table. Mom lifts a plate of chocolate chip cookies toward me. Melted chocolate covers her pink fingertips.

I wave the cookies away. "Mom, normally I'd scarf them down, but after my day, if I eat one of those, I'll puke. Got homework." I turn to hike up the stairs.

Halfway to my room, a chair scrapes against the hickory wood kitchen floor. With my foot on a step, I twist sideways. Mom's body stiffens as she rises. Her turquoise eyes fix on me. "Beth, where are your manners? Come back here. Take off your sunglasses and say hi to Mrs. Cummings."

I descend a few steps. My shades stay fixed. "Hi, Mrs. Cummings." Sticky sweet sarcasm.

A faint smile crosses the neighbor's face then fades. An uncomfortable silence blankets the room.

Mom shoots me a look. "I didn't expect you home yet. Doesn't track practice last until five thirty?"

A lump the size of a watermelon lodges in my throat. Yikes. Now I'll have to explain to the coach where I was and what happened. "Not today, Mom." I turn and schlep up the stairs to my room, feeling super, super miserable. I don't like how easily lying comes to me.

In my room, I insert a CD into the player and plop on my bed. Because I identify with the singer and understand his woes, I sing along. "Troubles keep multiplying and are driving me crazy. What should I do?" My answer is that I'm totally clueless.

I dress Friday morning and jump when horrible crashes come from downstairs in the kitchen. More clangs follow. I hurry down the stairs and stand in the doorway between the kitchen and the hall. Mom bends over two saucepan lids that litter the floor. I swallow a gulp. "Mom, are you okay?"

With the lids in her hands, she rises at my question. "Yes."

"It's a wonder the cops aren't rapping on the front door."

We share a quick smile. Then Mom says, "Covers slid off the saucepans and landed on the floor when I was putting away the microwave casserole dish that I used to make everyone's oatmeal." She bites her lip. "I have a seminar at the Red Lion Hotel for guidance counselors today and I'm not looking forward to it. Wish I could stay home." She blows out a puff and brushes a white strand of hair from her forehead. After placing the lids on their rightful owners, Mom walks across the kitchen floor and drops onto her seat with another breath.

Something's up. Mom normally has the energy of the stupid battery-operated bunny. I slide onto the chair between Stephanie and Mom and across from RC and reach for the sugar in the blue and white porcelain bowl. My arm brushes RC's hand as his fingertips stretch for and lightly touch his Spider-Man glass of milk. The glass tips and falls on the edge of his bowl and shatters. The comic book hero lands face up in RC's oatmeal. My brother's face turns a deep eggplant purple. Waves of tears flow from his caramel eyes. RC sobs and mumbles. "Sorry."

Mom hurries toward the refrigerator. "It's okay, RC. I'll get you another glass of milk and more food."

I lunge from my chair and help RC by mopping up the mess with napkins. After what happened yesterday, I completely understand what it feels like to be in an awkward situation.

Mom sets a glass of milk and oatmeal in front of RC. Then she sits, picks up the Mother of the Year mug that Robert bought her for Mother's Day, brings the brew to her mouth, and quickly sets the cup on the table.

"Coffee reject?" I ask.

"Yes. For some reason, it doesn't smell or taste good." After a silent moment, Mom drags her feet, wrapped in pink slippers, to the sink. She pours the coffee down the drain and stretches for the saltine cracker box on the third shelf of the cupboard. Then strolls back to the table with a fistful of wafers.

"What's up with the saltines?" I swallow a spoonful of porridge. "If you're getting the flu, keep your germs to yourself."

Steph and RC giggle then cover their faces.

Mom says, "Kids, I don't think it's anything contagious." She yawns, looks at her watch, and reminds us about her busy schedule.

I sniff the air. "What stinks?"

Mom hurries toward the smell, reaches for a pot holder, opens the door of the Toast-R-Oven, and turns on the fan. It hums and swallows a gulp of smoke. She picks up three black squares that resemble charcoal on a barbecue.

Stephanie pinches her nose. "Yuck."

"Sorry, kids," Mom says as she turns from the oven. "Got a lot on my mind."

I wave the smell of burnt toast away and hope that whatever Mom has on her mind won't amount to anything other than overcooked toast. "Would it be okay if I go over to Jimmy's after track practice? He wants me to help him with the antique car and stay for dinner."

Mom comes back to the table and sits. "Sure, go ahead. I'm glad the two of you have a good time together."

"Thanks. We do."

Mom rests her hand on my arm. "Beth, I need you to take Steph and RC to school."

I choke then clear my throat. "Again? Drove them every day last week." Some days, I wonder if she wants to trade her Mom Badge in for an "I'm Busy—Don't Bother Me" button.

"I know and I do thank you. But Robert and I depend on you as the oldest to help out from time to time." Mom gathers dirty dishes and musters enough strength to march to the sink.

"Mom, Steph and RC are not my kids. I said I'd help out once in a while, but I have a schedule to keep too."

Steph jumps up. Her bounce resembles Tiger when she's excited. "Beth, take me to school, won't you? Won't you?"

There have been moments when I've had trouble understanding my sister. She always seems to want to be on my good side so the sitter will take her where she wants to go. When I'm heading out to the mall, Steph asks if she can tag along. It gets on my nerves. Maybe she just wants closeness. Maybe big sisters are supposed to understand, but right now I could care less.

RC raises his hand, but before he's able to share his thoughts… the phone rings. Mom turns her head from the dishwasher. "Beth, please get that. Jot down the name and number and tell him or her that I'll call back this evening."

I stand, click my heels, salute, and pick up the receiver. "Hello, this is Beth. Good morning to you too, Mrs. Anderson. I'm fine. No, Mom's busy right now. Can I take a message?" I open the junk drawer, find an old receipt, and scribble the message. "I'll tell Mom you called. Bye." I hang up and slap the receipt on the counter. "Mrs. Anderson wants to know if you'll have coffee with her after work. Guess you won't be doing that, huh?"

I return to what we were talking about before the phone interrupted. "Mom, this babysitting thing is turning into more than once in a while. A nanny usually gets paid."

My commander dries her hands and plants them on her narrow hips.

I understand her unsmiling, concentrated glare. "Okay, okay, I'll do it." I look at Stephanie and RC. "Come on kids, let's go to school."

❋ ❋ ❋

After I drop the kids off at their school, my day is a ho-hum routine for which I should be grateful. I hustle toward the gym lockers after English Lit and change into my running gear. Wearing sunscreen and my Dodgers baseball cap, I run outside and see Coach Forsythe standing in the middle of the football field.

The coach's words echo across the field. "Okay, teams gather round." I jog over and stand in front of the coach.

After all are assembled, the coach asks, "Where's Brian?"

Molly says, "Dunno."

Brian is a jazz musician and it keeps him busy.

The coach continues. "Molly and Susan, meet with Coach Stevenson. He'll give you instructions for your sprint workouts." He turns to Jimmy, Josh, and me. "Start today's distance practice with drills, stretches, and a fifteen-minute run. After that, come back for further instructions."

In unison, Jimmy, Josh, and I turn and head toward the track that surrounds the field.

Coach calls me back. "Beth, wait up."

I stop and turn around and run back to the coach.

"What happened yesterday? Missed you at practice."

"Sorry. Had a really bad day." Because yesterday was so horrible and unmentionable, I *really* couldn't face Coach and more questions.

"Is there anything you want to talk about?"

"Nope."

I catch up with Susan just before she joins Molly and Coach Stevenson on the far side of the field. Her slender six-foot frame, along with her muscular thighs and long legs, gives her the explosive power she needs to jump the one-hundred-meter hurdles, her passion. "Suze, do you think you'll qualify for the prelims?"

Susan stretches a hamstring and shields her eyes from the hot California sun. "Hope so. I saw in the paper that some girl ran the hurdles in 11.43. I want to beat that time. How about you? You ready to run the 800 and the 3,200?"

"Sure. I've been running every day. And, like you, I want to beat the records for my races too. I'm pumped."

"Good luck," Susan waves and runs off.

I join the guys for stretches and the quick run. Jimmy asks, "How's it been going since we met at lunch? Are you still fuming about taking the kids to school for the sixth time?"

I swat a bee. "No. I'm over it. Until it happens again."

The guys share a short laugh. Josh slows to a walk. "At my house, with four younger siblings, it gets to be a drag when I have to cart my two brothers and two sisters to where they need to go. Schedules get pretty messed up. If you come over, prepare to wear your battle gear. It's as busy as JFK Airport."

Jimmy and I laugh aloud.

"Well," Jimmy says, "I wish I had some siblings. Being the only kid can be lonely."

I'm quiet but ponder the idea that maybe he should count himself lucky. The three of us finish our run and sprint over to the coach.

Coach Forsythe says, "Jimmy and Josh run four quick fifty-meter sprints, rotate two times between four-hundred- and eight-hundred-meter intervals with two minutes recovery time, and finish up with an easy five miles. Don't forget to cool down."

I wait for instruction while the coach watches Jimmy and Josh jog toward the track. Then Coach turns my way. "Beth, after you practice for your eight-hundred-meter race today, I want you to do a hard run for five miles. Finish your workout with a ten-minute cool down and stretches. On Monday, I'll help you prepare for the 3,200-meter event."

I blow out a puff of warm air. "Okay, Coach." I run off with thoughts about my time with Jimmy in the garage.

Following practice, I drive to Jimmy's house and pull onto his driveway. Jimmy is in the open garage perched on the hood of the Chevy in his paint-spotted and oil-stained white T-shirt and blue jeans. I open my car door. "Hey, Jimmy."

"Hey, yourself," Jimmy says as he jumps onto the concrete and runs over to me.

"Anything new?" I ask.

"Yeah. Tell you in a minute. Let's get inside. It's about fifteen degrees cooler in the garage."

After following Jimmy into the garage, Jimmy flips the switch to lower the garage door. When the door is down, Jimmy gives his chin scruff a thoughtful scratch. Then he meanders his way around the car to the graying rough-wood workbench and snatches two pieces of sandpaper from underneath an auto mechanic manual. And then he wheels around and gets back to answering my question. "After lunch today, I registered for the SAT."

I sit on the cold concrete next to the side of the car. Staring at an unpolished spot, I ask, "Why didn't you tell me at practice?"

Jimmy sits next to me and hands me one of the pieces of rough paper. "Because I was waiting for our time together. My goal is to go prelaw."

I know he works at his father's law office after track practice two or three days a week. I thought it was money for pleasure and entertainment. Never thought it might be a career choice.

I say, "Wow," then swallow a hard lump.

Of course he'd join the other college-bound students after graduation. He's too smart not to. We're not dating so it shouldn't matter where he goes to college. But I ask, "Prelaw studies where?"

"Biola. It's a Christian university in La Mirada. About an hour drive from here. My parents are going to take me to visit the campus this summer."

I wrinkle my nose. "It's none of my business, but I've heard that Bible thumpin' girls are, you know, snobs."

Jimmy laughs. "Maybe some of them are, Beth. But I'm not going to college to be around girls. I get enough of that here."

I stand. "*Excuse* me. Is that a hint for me to take off?"

"Just kidding. Sit down and let me finish." Jimmy waits to continue until I sit. Then he says, "God says in His Word to not be anxious about anything, so I'm praying about it. Will you miss me?"

"Miss you? Please." I pick up a red polishing cloth and throw it at his chest. If I told him my true feelings, my dream of dating him, would he change his mind?

Jimmy throws the cloth back. "If I go, I'll miss you, Beth. We've still got our senior year to look forward to. Right now, let's finish sanding this last coat of primer."

I rub a spot with sandpaper. "If you go, won't you miss your mom…your dad…the time in the garage?" Memories of Daddy flood my brain at the strangest times.

Jimmy buffs a rough spot. "Sure, I'll miss my parents." He studies me.

I lay the paper down and stare at the cold concrete. "My dad—"

He stops working. "You told me in middle school."

"Sorry."

"Don't be sorry, Beth. Please, continue."

Tears cloud my eyes. I grab a soiled rag, clench it in my fist, and stare at a grease spot. "Sorry for bringing it up again, but after seeing and hearing about your good relationship with your father, it makes me miss mine all over again. After Daddy left, Mom expected me to move on."

Jimmy inches closer and catches my falling tear with the edge of his shirt. "Do you remember a good time that you had with your dad?"

"Yes. One day before work, he kissed me goodbye and lifted me high in the air and asked, 'Who flies like a bird? Who can go anywhere?'"

"Don't stop, Beth."

"I giggled, 'Daddy, me.' Then he twirled me around."

Jimmy pulls me closer.

I relax into his warm arms. My head rests underneath the curve of his chin. I cry.

Jimmy whispers, "It's okay to cry. I've never experienced a loss like that. I don't know what to say, except that I'll be here for you. And I'll pray for you."

I push away and stare into his eyes. "You think prayer works?"

"Yes."

"I had a bad experience with prayer, Jimmy. I don't believe it does any good."

Jimmy's bushy brows knit. "Tell me why, Beth."

After a deep breath, I release another part of my pent-up pain. "One day, when I was little, Grandma Bma sat on her rocker and called me to come and sit on her lap. Her gentle arms wrapped around me; her wrinkled arthritic fingers stroked my hair. And her false teeth clicked when she whispered, 'Beth, I pray for you always. Don't ever forget that God hears our prayers.' Then Bma hugged me. My head rested on her bony shoulder.

"Bma took me to church and Sunday school. Mom stayed home. Everyone looked so happy. I wanted to be like them.

"The Sunday school teacher, Miss Marvel, said, 'Jesus loves you.' Then she emphasized the words by pointing her finger to each of the kids, including me, seated on the floor in front of her.

"Weeks later, Miss Marvel continued with her lesson. 'Jesus knows and cares about everything that happens in our lives. When you are happy, He is happy. And when you are sad, well—He's sad too. Jesus lives in Heaven now. But He did live, die, and rise from the grave. He lived for forty days. Then Jesus was taken up into Heaven. If you invite Jesus to come and live in your heart, someday, you can live with Him forever in Heaven.' She looked around the room and asked, 'Is there anyone who would like to invite Jesus to come into their heart?'

"I had the uncomfortable feeling that her Hershey's Milk Chocolate eyes saw my pain. After minutes of silence, my hand shot up in the air. Miss Marvel prayed for me and gave me two gifts—a hug and a Bible."

"Where's your Bible today?"

"Give me a minute. I'll explain." I blow out a long sigh and continue. "I read the Bible for a while with the teacher and Bma. Then

Bma died. Then I was not only angry with God for never bringing Daddy back but furious because He had no prob taking Bma from me. So God and I aren't speaking. Prefer to keep it that way. My thought is that it makes God happier because it frees Him up to concentrate on someone else. But my pain and questions mount. Today, the Bible sits on my dresser collecting dust."

Jimmy puts his arm around my shoulders. "Bad things do happen, and we don't understand why a loving God would allow such pain. But trust me. God knows about your pain. In the Bible, the Israelites grew restless when they didn't see God solving their immediate problems. We become like them when we think God doesn't love us or when His answer is delayed."

I rest my back against the door of the car and chew on a splintered nail.

Jimmy continues. "I know God loves you, Beth. And I think you're all right too."

Silence.

"Beth, let's finish sanding and spray on another coat of primer. Dinner should be ready soon."

Chapter 3

After dinner and a walk with Jimmy, I push open the front door and step inside at nine thirty and find Robert and Mom sitting at the kitchen table. Robert looks up from his magazine and then quickly returns his eyes to what he was supposedly reading. Mom asks, "Did you and Jimmy have fun?"

I plop down on the chair next to Mom. "Yeah, we finished sanding one coat and put on another coat of primer. Had pot roast, gravy, carrots, potatoes, and a salad with every fresh vegetable imaginable. Then Jimmy's mom brought out a homemade Dutch apple pie for dessert." I swallow. "It was so good." I wrap a strand of brown shoulder-length hair around my finger and think.

Think about how Mom used to be an excellent cook. She cooked pot roast, but her homemade spaghetti sauce was to die for. Before Robert and the kids came along, Mom was a Julia Child wannabe. One time, I counted twenty five cookbooks on the shelf in the pantry. But that's history because now Mom is busy and tired. All we do is eat and run.

I rise from the chair and kiss Mom on the cheek with, "I love you" and hurry up to my room. In my room, my head rests against the pillow. I pick up my journal and write:

> Good news is that I got an A on the geometry test. Found out that Jimmy's interested in Biola. Selfishly I hope he doesn't get in. I'd miss his friendship. I told Jimmy about Daddy. He said he would pray for me. Ugh. Like that will help.

I mark the page, close the book, stare at my chewed, uneven nails, and turn off the light.

Mom shakes me awake. "Beth, I've let you sleep in."

"What time is it?"

"Eight o'clock."

"You call eight a sleep in?"

Mom says, "I have to be at work by nine. I need you to take Stephanie to dance lessons and watch RC."

Anger bubbles in my throat like lava in a volcano. I throw off the blue chenille blanket and sit up. "No fair. I took Steph and RC to school yesterday. It's Saturday. I was planning on calling Molly to see if we could get in on some sales."

"I know it's Saturday, Beth. After the seminar, I went to the office to retrieve my emails and got a message from a girl who was in a state of crisis so I committed to see her this morning." Mom says as she walks toward the door, "I'll be home by three. Then you can call Molly. Hurry. The kids need you."

The door closes.

I spit, "Hurry, hurry, hurry," under my breath. Mom knows the word "hurry" well. Maybe she's responsible for putting it into Webster's.

Annoyed, I push my feet into my oversize Mickey Mouse slippers and stomp down the stairs and tear into the kitchen. Half dressed in black pants, pink robe, and hair in curlers, Mom pulls milk from the fridge. After seeing me, she lays the container on the counter and rests her back against the hardwood cabinets with arms folded, modeling authority. Our eyes meet.

I slap my hands on my hips. "Mom, I don't get it. You own the business. You could've told the girl that you'd meet her later in the day. Steph's class doesn't start until ten. If you call the girl now and change the time for this afternoon, you can still keep your appointment. I'll get my day. We both win."

"No, Beth. I need to catch up on paperwork. I've fed the kids. Your breakfast is on the table."

Feeling defeated, I drop my hands to my sides, walk toward the table, and sit on my chair. Mom joins me. "I'll give you money so you can treat the kids to lunch and stop at the store to pick up bread and milk."

I shriek. "What? Now I have to take them to lunch and shop for groceries?"

She raises her voice a few decibels. "Yes, you do. And you'd better change your tone, young lady, or you won't be going anywhere."

I fire back. "Mom, what's wrong with my attitude?"

"You're being selfish."

"Selfish?"

Mom throws me her controlling-mom look.

"Okay." I stab the microwaved scrambled eggs with my fork, take a bite, and spit the cold yellow clumps in a napkin.

Mom pulls thirty dollars from her robe pocket and slides the money my way. I tap the money with my forefinger. My thoughts—here, there, everywhere. "Can't Robert watch the kids?"

"Robert's not here. Last night he got a frantic call from flight personnel asking him to stand in for another pilot who became ill. He won't be home until after eight." She swallows and continues. "We've discussed this long enough. Steph's in the living room watching cartoons, and your brother is playing in his room and doesn't want to get dressed. Deal with it, Beth." She pulls a curler from her head, stands, and marches out of the kitchen.

Stephanie skates across the kitchen's polished wood floor in her stocking feet and stands in front of me. "Mom said you're going to take me to dance lessons."

"Yeah. Got roped again."

Steph hangs her head and runs toward the living room. Just before she makes it back to the hall carpet, her feet go under her. Stephanie bumps her forehead against the doorframe. She wails and raises her hand to her head. She screams again after seeing dark crimson on her hand.

I examine the injury. "Don't cry, Steph. The wound is small." I grab a clean napkin off the table and press it hard against her cut. "Don't think we need to call 911. Steph, let's go upstairs and get a bandage." I plant a kiss on the top of her head.

Our arms resemble links on a chain as we climb the steps and head for emergency services in the bathroom. Feeling like a nurse, I perform surgery by applying Neosporin and a Band-Aid to the injured site.

Stephanie swipes two standing tears with the back of her hand. "Thank you, Beth."

"Glad to be of service, Steph."

After I emerge from urgent care with my sister, Mom, with hair combed and fully dressed, meets us in the hallway. "What happened?"

Stephanie turns and hugs me. "I fell and bumped my head. Nurse Beth took care of it."

"Thanks, Beth," Mom says as she tosses a wink my way.

Steph skips to her room like she never got hurt.

At eight forty-five, Mom dashes down the stairs. The front door shuts with a "bang."

RC comes around the corner with Legos in his hand. "Where's Mommy?"

"Gone to work. I'm in charge. I have to take Steph to dance lessons and you have to go with me."

RC disappears. My Smart phone buzzes. I run from the hallway, jump on my unmade bed and recognize the lit number. "Hey, Molly."

"Whatcha doing today?"

"I've got unexpected KP duty."

"What's KP duty?"

"Kid patrol."

"That's a bummer. I was calling to see if you'd go shopping."

"Molly, funny thing that you called because I was going to call you later to ask the same thing. Mom promised to be home by three. Could we go shopping when she gets home?"

"No, Beth. Won't work for me. Abercrombie & Fitch at the Galleria Mall is having a sale, and I want to be there when they open.

I should be home by the time you are free. But call just in case. I'll show you my new stuff." Then Molly adds, "Later," and abruptly hangs up.

Molly's favorite stores are Abercrombie & Fitch for sweaters and jeans and Macy's for accessories and shoes. The creative way that she puts outfits together amazes me. I like Macy's but am not so into fashion. Looking for clothes is retail therapy for me because I'm able to sweep life's troubles under the carpet for an hour or two.

I kick piles of clothes on the floor until my black T-shirt and denim shorts drift to the top. I grumble, "The sale lasts all day. She could've waited." Disgusted that the day isn't going as I planned, I slide my feet into my flip-flops, tie my hair in a loose knot, and head for Steph's room.

When I enter the room. Steph pulls peppermint pink tights and a black licorice leotard out of the dresser drawer. "Steph, pack a change of clothes because after dance class we're getting burgers and stopping for groceries."

I walk to RC's room. He's still in his Spider-Man PJs. He sits crisscross applesauce on the bedroom floor and appears lost in an imaginary world while creating something out of Legos.

RC looks up.

"It's time to stop playing, RC. Get dressed."

RC snaps another Lego into place.

I kneel and put a hand on his. "RC, did you hear what I said?"

"Can I go to Tommy's?" RC cocks his head and stares at me with his brown eyes as big as ET's saucer.

"No, RC. Mom said to take you with me. Maybe you can go to Tommy's when she comes home." I soften my voice and rest my hand on his shoulder. "Get dressed. Please. We need to be at Steph's dance class by nine thirty."

Exhausted from the mental game of ping pong with my brother, I run to the bathroom to gather my thoughts. I inhale and exhale deeply.

Just as I let out a breath, the pictures on the walls and towels on the rods shake and resemble the side effects of an earthquake. I throw open the door to investigate. I discover that it's not a trembling of the earth's crust, but Steph and RC's feet as they scramble down the stairs and head for the car.

"Thank you, kids. I'll buy ice cream after lunch."

✳ ✳ ✳

After dance class, lunch, and the store, I—with Steph and RC in tow—arrive home. I anxiously wait for Mom to show up. She opens the front door at four o'clock, an hour late. I punch in Molly's number.

Molly answers with a breathless "Hello" on the third ring.

"Hey, you sound winded. Did you just get home?"

"Yeah. Had a terrific day because Mom came with me when you couldn't."

Envy clings to me like raspberry jam on bread when I remember the duel I had with Mom this morning.

"Are you free now?" Molly asks.

"Yeah."

"Good. Come over. Can't wait to show you what I bought."

"Okay. Be there in a few. Bye." I drive to Molly's house a half mile away, park on her driveway, exit, and hurry toward the backdoor screen. Then standing in front of the screen and open door I see Molly next to the counter. Whiffs of melted chocolate float my way. "Hey, Molly."

She turns her head. "Come in, Beth."

An ocean of saliva forms in my mouth when I step into the kitchen and spot two opened Cokes standing on the white-tile countertop and paper napkins holding brownies with dark chocolate frosting.

Molly points. "This okay?"

"More than okay. Thanks." I follow Molly to her room and drop down on the beige plush carpet and take a swig of my Coke.

Molly bends her knees to sit. But before she gets all the way to the floor, her cell sings from the other side of the room. She straightens, turns, and runs toward the ring. "Hey Josh. What's on your mind? No, can't. Beth's here. Maybe after she leaves."

I pucker my lips, narrow my eyes, and stand. "Do you want me to take off?"

She motions for me to sit and then turns her back, whispering. I grab an issue of *Seventeen Magazine,* sit on her bed and flip pages. Molly screams. "Of course. I'll go to the dance with you next Saturday." With her arms extended in dance position, she flies around the room like Tinkerbelle.

The bouncing and spinning makes me laugh but feel sick at the same time.

"I'll call you later, Josh. Bye." Molly folds the phone and spins around. I look up. "Beth, do you have a date for the dance?"

"Not yet."

"Think you'll get asked?"

"Well—Jimmy and I are friends. We hang out after practices."

Molly's eyebrows shoot toward the skylight. She covers her mouth and laughs through her fingers, "Think he'll ask you?"

I stand. "Don't know. But it would be nice."

"I think it's highly unlikely that Jimmy will ask you, Beth."

"Why would you say such a thing, Molly?"

"I can't see you with Jimmy. Because he seems like he's got no problems and has life all figured out and you—"

I glare at her. "What are you trying to say? Spit it out."

Molly plants her feet like they've been rooted for 2,200 years like General Sherman, the world's tallest sequoia tree in California. She holds her breath for a second and then, with a pointed jaw, blurts out everything on her mind. "Okay, you asked for it. FYI, Beth. You have everything, but you continue to whine about your problem. How is Jimmy dealing with it?"

I'm speechless for a sec. Then decide to not to let her get away with what she just dished out, I say. "Molly, like I told you I don't know why my dad left, and I struggle with not having the answers. I have talked with Jimmy about it. And because we're friends he listens. Thought you and I were friends and we could talk about anything. What's going on?"

"We're still friends, just a different kind."

"And what kind is that?"

"Forget it, Beth." Molly says as she walks toward the closet. "Want to see my clothes or not?"

Totally miffed at the quick change of subjects, I leave my half-eaten brownie and full bottle of Coke on the floor and follow Molly. She opens the doors to her walk-in closet and exposes tees, tanks, and sandals with expensive price tags still attached. Her lips turn up into an enormous grin resembling those of a Cheshire cat.

I move next to her and stare at the clothes. "You sure made a haul." Not wanting to stick around because I'm frustrated with Molly and the half hour that I spent with her, I flip open my cell and check the time. "Gotta go, Molly. Catch ya later."

My thought—*it will be a very long time before I spend any time with her.* I zip down the stairs and head for Molly's back door.

Chapter 4

S till thinking about Molly's spiteful words, I stand trembling on the sidewalk adjacent to her screen door. I decide to go for a run in the park to get rid of my irritation before heading home. I sprint over to my car, jump in, and turn on the engine. Then back out of Molly's driveway and put my car in drive. I step on the throttle. My tires screech around the corner.

Red lights flash in my rearview mirror. *Oh no. Not today, not now.*

With my hands shaking faster than leaves in a windstorm, I pull over to the side and stop. A policeman approaches. Now, not only peeved with Molly, I'm mad about my trouble with the law. I roll down the window. Tears cloud my vision.

The lawman says, "Good afternoon, young lady. I'm Sergeant Hoffman from the Glendale Police Department. Do you have your license and registration?"

Shaking, I nod and pass all identification to the Arnold Schwarzenegger look-alike.

Sergeant Hoffman says, "Did you know you were doing fifty in a twenty-five-mile-per-hour zone?"

My only option is to lie. "Sorry, officer. Didn't realize. Just came from the hospital and found out"—I scoop up the Kleenex box sitting next to me and pluck tissues, then compose myself—"found out that I'm really sick." My lying is off the charts. "Officer, I won't do it again." I wail and sink my face in another tissue. "I promise."

"I'm sorry that you're sick, but if I catch you cruising over the limit again, the ticket will be two hundred dollars or more. I'll let you off with a warning this time." He hands me a ticket with the word "warning" printed in bold letters.

"Thank you. Thank you." I dry my tears and blow my nose. "I promise it won't happen again. May I go now?"

"Yes. Just remember, miss, that you are supposed to keep your speed at twenty five in a residential area. I'll pray for you."

"Thank you." Hating myself for lying, I roll up the window. I wave as the kind officer drives by. I tell myself not to tell anyone about the run-in with the law. If the incident gets out, it would be JJN (juicy, juicy news). Could even hit the gossip column of *Explosion*, the school newspaper, or float to Molly's ears.

I wipe my tears, then take in breaths and let them out slowly, trying to calm my nerves. Too shook up, I forgo a run in the park and wait quietly until my heart rate slows to normal.

After thirty minutes, I turn on the engine, gently step on the gas pedal, and watch my speedometer on my way home.

※ ※ ※

My mouth instantly waters at the smell of beef. "Mom, what's for dinner?"

Mom turns her head and wipes a brow. "Tacos. Something easy. I'm not feeling well."

"What's the matter?"

"My stomach's still upset. Would you help?"

"Okay."

"Get the tomatoes out of the fridge and chop them up." She reaches into the cupboard, hands me a bowl, turns on the fan above the stove, and stirs the browning beef sirloin.

I grab six tomatoes, put them on the chopping block, and get a knife from the drawer. "Mom, last week, Mr. Max wanted to know if I was going to sit for the SAT. Told him maybe."

"Beth, why did you tell him that? Of course, you'll take it."

"Because—I don't know what I want to do." I sweep the chopped vegetables into the bowl with my open palm, rip a paper towel from the roll, and wipe up red juice that splashed on the floor. "I was hoping we could talk about it—and other things."

Mom holds up her hand like a traffic cop at an intersection. Then she runs to the bathroom and leaves the door ajar. She coughs.

35

The toilet flushes. Her footsteps are faintly heard on the stairs as she makes her way up to her room.

I finish cooking the meat, assemble the ingredients, and call the kids for dinner, explaining that I'm in charge until their father comes home. Stephanie and RC wolf down the meal and dash back to what I suspect is their television program.

The back door swings open. My stepfather walks in. "Hi, Beth. Where's your mom?"

"Mom got sick. Think she went to bed. I fed the kids. They're in the living room watching the boob tube. How was your day? Sorry your plane was delayed. I bet you're tired."

Showing no hints of sticking around, Robert's trench coat drags on the floor behind him as he crosses the entry and heads for the living room. Screams of delight come from the other room. "Daddy's home! Daddy's home!"

I peek around the corner and watch Robert lift RC into his arms. Stephanie waits for her turn with the body language of an excited tail-wagging puppy. The scene brings back memories of my times with Daddy. I wipe a tear.

After hugs, my stepdad sits on the couch and puts a kid on each knee. All three laugh in unison at something funny on the screen. Then during a commercial, Robert gives each child a loving pat. "Kids, finish watching your program, then I'll read you a bedtime story. Right now, I need to check on your mom."

Robert comes my way and passes me. Then with his foot on the first step, he apparently has second thoughts because he twists around and loosens his tie. "How was your day, Beth?"

Even though his question is delayed, I choose to forgive the guy. Worried that he's in a hurry, I jam the day's events together. "Took Steph to dance lessons, went to Molly's for a while—not good. We have a track meet next Satur—"

I don't get to finish because Robert turns, climbs the remaining stairs, and disappears around the corner. I lean against the doorframe, sad.

When the sun lights up my room like fireworks over Times Square on the Fourth of July, I hope it will not be another boring Sunday. In the past, it's been the norm for Mom and Robert to sleep in. The kids watch cartoons, and I'm left to fend for myself.

I walk over to the open window, sit on the floor, and lean against the frame. Tree swallows chirp, whine, and gurgle. I laugh as they zip through the air, acrobatically twisting and turning their deep blue iridescent backs and clean white fronts. I greet them right back with, "And good morning to you too. Maybe something will happen so I can be excited about this day too." I throw on my robe and open the door a crack. It's weird that the television is not blaring.

I step into the hallway to check things out; Robert comes around the corner. "Beth, your mom's still sick. The kids are sleeping in. Do what you want today, but write a note if you leave, okay?"

"Sure." I retreat to my room wondering how Mom got this bug.

My cell phone sings with contemporary Christian music. My heart skips a beat. I jump across piles. "Hi, Jimmy."

"Beth, I was wondering if you'd go to service with me this morning. We could grab lunch afterward."

"Haven't been in a long, long time, Jimmy, but my stepdad just told me that I could do anything that I wanted today, so sure." I'm willing to risk anything to get out of the house and be with Jimmy.

"Great. I'll pick you up in a half hour."

"I'll be ready. Bye."

After showering, I stand in front of the closet and chew on a nail. I settle on a white cotton shirt with pearl buttons, yellow and blue printed skirt, and metallic strappy sandals and examine myself in the full-length mirror. It will be great for this cloudless spring day. Next, I scrounge around on the floor for my white purse, brush my hair in a knot, and fly out of the bedroom with pearl earrings in hand. Halfway down the stairs I halt, turn back around, and dash back. I dust the Bible with yesterday's T-shirt, fly down the stairs, and head for the kitchen.

I lay the Bible on the kitchen table and scan the counter for something to write on. I scribble a note on a paper napkin with a felt pen from the junk drawer. "Went to church with Jimmy. Be home later. Beth."

Jimmy knocks on the front door. "Hi, I'm ready."

"Wow, you look fabulous."

"Thanks, Jimmy."

Today, he is looking handsome in his black dress pants, white T-shirt, and blue blazer. The sport coat highlights his eyes.

"What made you invite me to church?"

We walk toward Jimmy's car. "After you shared your pain on Friday, I thought it might help." He holds the passenger door of his white Honda Civic open. "And this morning, I sensed God wanted me to ask you. I'm glad you accepted. I think you'll like Pastor Rosenburg and the youth group." He flashes a grin.

I gather my skirt and step in. "How long have you been going to First Baptist?"

A minute later Jimmy jumps in behind the wheel. "What's your pleasure, Beth, window or air conditioner?"

"Let's go air conditioner."

"You got it." Jimmy powers up the windows, dials the switch for air on low, and backs out of the driveway. "My parents started taking me when I was young. I've always gone. It's what I want to do and need to do. Plus, there are a lot of neat people there. We all have hurts, and when others share their hurts, well…all is good. When you meet the youth group, you'll understand."

Jimmy and I jaw about restoring the car and school this coming week. I ask, "Are you ready for the track meet on Saturday?"

He turns his head. "Yeah. I'm pumped. Some guy ran the 3,200 meters on the varsity team in eight minutes, fifty-five seconds. I think I can beat his time. Are you ready for your races?"

"Think so. Sure would like to beat my past times."

"You're so determined, Beth. If you keep working, I know you'll do it because I believe in you." Jimmy winks.

"Thanks."

Jimmy swings into the parking lot of the First Baptist Church of Glendale. He opens my car door, escorts me toward the front, and opens the double white doors. The pastor stands to the side of entrance. Jimmy and the minister shake hands.

The Pastor says, "Jimmy, I'm glad to see you on this fine Sunday. Who is this young lady?"

Jimmy wraps his arm around my waist. "It's my pleasure, Pastor Rosenburg, to introduce you to my friend Beth Paine."

Even though my heart rate increases and a coppery taste floods my mouth and I feel warm, I shake the pastor's hand and give him my best smile.

"Nice to meet you, Beth. Glad you could join us today."

"Thanks."

Jimmy turns toward a yell. "Hey, Jimmy, over here."

My friend cups his hand around my elbow and guides me over to a group gathered in the corner. "Hi, guys. This is Beth Paine. Beth, this is Ty Schmidt, James Ramey, Matthew Powell, and Carol Miner."

Carol's wave resembles windshield wipers on high speed.

I ask, "Carol, didn't we have some sophomore classes together?"

"Yes."

Following the introductions, everyone greets me with slaps of acceptance. Jimmy jumps back in. "You can meet the rest of the gang later."

Ty piggybacks on Jimmy's plan to get me involved immediately. "Yeah, come to the youth group. We need new blood."

I think, *Let's not rush it*, but promise myself to consider it because my fears about being treated like an alien are completely unsound.

We all file into the sanctuary and sit together on a pew. The pastor approaches the pulpit after three long songs. He sets a water glass on the raised platform, opens his Bible, and clears his throat. "Tonight's sermon is called, 'I Have a Plan.'" After a moment he proceeds. "God has a plan for each of us. We must trust God for each step, pray, and let Him have control."

I let God have control once and He botched it up. But today it feels like God's still tapping me on the shoulder. I feel numb—it's a numbness I can't explain.

After an hour, the pastor concludes his sermon. "Now go in peace, and if anyone has any questions, I'll be in the foyer. The grace of our Lord Jesus Christ be with you all."

I remain seated. The group files out. Jimmy turns to me. "What did you think about the sermon?"

Because I have a million, trillion wild questions, my lips remain sealed. "Where are we going for lunch? I'm starving."

When Jimmy drops me off at home around four thirty I thank him for the invite, lunch, popcorn, and the movie. *Did he really mean it when he said that there will be other times like today? Is he going to ask me to the prom?*

I wave and shut the door. The refrigerator hums. Afraid that this silence will suddenly erupt with voices and demands, I creep up the stairs to my room, change into my running outfit, and bolt out the front door. Before I hit the sidewalk, I screech to a halt and turn around. I leave the front door ajar and head for the kitchen table. The floor creaks. The grandfather clock echoes five chimes. I freeze. Seconds pass. I tip toe and add a postscript to the note I wrote hours before. "Went to the park."

Chapter 5

I drive beside a sign that reads, "Griffith Park" and take in a deep breath. The surroundings, peaceful. The yellow glow of the sun's ray splashes on tall green pine trees as they sway to and fro in the breeze. Vibrant colors of lemon drop yellow, raspberry red, peppermint pink, and marshmallow white adorn rhododendron bushes that are sprinkled throughout the grounds like sugar on a confection treat. I pass a crystal clear lake and watch ducks glide in unison. The car idles. A man and a young boy stand on the embankment and cast a line into the pond. I draw in another breath and let it out. Maybe someday, I can have peace like the scene I see. A peace that will not be just for a time but a lasting one.

I move on and slip into a parking slot. Then I turn off the engine and get out. I stroll over to a brook that bubbles over moss laden rocks. I think about the never-ending verbal battles with Mom, my dislike of Robert, the Molly problem, the upcoming SAT test, and fears about the future. I sob, wanting things to be different.

A weather-beaten dull gray bench beckons me to sit. After sitting, I notice smooth brown wood has taken the place of gray paint on the armrests—elbow wear, I suspect. I find comfort in the fact that others found this to be a nook of tranquility. My shoulders relax and droop.

Pastor Rosenburg's words echo through my head. "Let God have control." Why can't I shake the sermon? His words?

I sigh. In my peripheral vision, my eyes spot a dull blue-gray suitcase beneath the slats of my bench. I'm tempted to pull it out, but I have second thoughts. *The suitcase could have a bomb inside it. Should I call the cops?* Because it looks safe, I cautiously pull it out and pick it up. Traveling stickers decorate the sides. A note has been attached under the handle and addressed to "Friend."

I open the envelope and take out the note and read:

Dear Friend, I'm so glad you found my suitcase. I want to share it with you. Let love take you everywhere you go and through each situation. I've lived for many years and the decades have presented different coats for me to wear.

I've worn the battle scars of pain, fear, hate, and anger just to name a few. But also with those I claim love, joy, peace, patience, kindness, goodness, faithfulness, gentleness, and self-control. The latter have carried me.

The contents will cause you to reminisce, but don't be afraid. Hold onto the recollections that strengthen you and let go of the ones that confine you like a prisoner in a cell. But, embrace each memory. You will learn from each and come to understand yourself.

And the traveling stickers, well—they serve as a reminder to you and to me that there are many roads that we must travel. Sometimes you will feel like skipping in the sunshine and other times you will wonder how you'll get through the dark valley. But you don't have to travel alone; it's up to you. My friend, travel life's journey with adventure in mind. Learn, grow. I'll be praying for you. God bless.

Tears make what feels like highways down my cheeks. In one swift motion, I wipe the water with my forearm and glance at a postscript. There's no signature but the P.S reads:

When you've finished examining the contents and the memories that they bring, you might want to add something from your life to encourage another. Then, gently close the lid and place it back where you found it. Remember…it only takes a spark to get a fire going.

What does fire have to do with anything? I'll ask Jimmy in the morning. Maybe, he'll know the answer.

The sun rests on the horizon. Intrigued by the mystery of the suitcase and its contents, I head for home with the letter in one hand and the suitcase in the other.

I open the back door. Mom stands on the other side. "Beth, I was going to send Robert out to look for you." She swings the door all the way open and then slaps her hands on her hips. "It's late. We're about to have dinner. Where have you been?"

"Didn't you get my note?"

"Robert and I looked all over and finally found an illegible ink-smeared note lying on the kitchen floor."

"Sorry, Mom. The note said I was going to church with Jimmy. Then I added a postscript later telling you that I was going to the park. That's where I've been. The paper napkin was the only thing I could find."

Mom and Robert's facial expressions—masklike.

"I put the note on the table. The writing was clear when I wrote it. Maybe one of the kids splashed water on the words." I giggle, then continue. "A warm breeze from the open window probably blew it onto the floor. Sorry."

"Make sure that the notes you write in the future are legible and visible," Mom says as she walks toward the sink with a worn gray hand towel over her shoulder.

Still gripping my finds, I follow her retreating back. "Glad you are better. Look what I found. There's a letter that seems full of code too. Want to read it with me?"

"Thank you for caring. I'm still a little nauseous. I'll look at what you've got later." She reaches for a glass, fills it with water, takes a sip, and then wheels around. "Right now, go wash your hands and come to the table. Stephanie and RC are hungry."

My joy deflates faster than a helium balloon lets out gas. Frustrated, I tear off a splintered nail with my teeth. Wondering if Mom's time to look at my find will be soon or later or forgotten.

During dinner, Stephanie complains about too much homework. Mom reminds RC that unless he eats his peas, there won't be dessert. Bored with the conversation, I finish my meal and head up to my room to work on homework. After tomorrow's assignments are completed, I slip between the sheets and wonder, *What's so great about the contents in the suitcase that someone would care enough to leave them for me?*

❇ ❇ ❇

I wake Monday morning before six. My emotions—here, there, everywhere. Excited and nervous about the contents in the suitcase. I opt to wait until tonight to unveil the first item. I realize that trying to go back to sleep is pointless.

My stomach rumbles. Understanding the internal code for "feed me," I throw on my robe, tie my hair in a loose knot, and run down the stairs.

In the kitchen, I run my palm over the sleeping microwave and stare at it. I decide to make breakfast and give the electric oven a break. When great ideas pop out from nowhere, it blows me away. I slap a skillet on the stove and gather bacon and eggs from the fridge. Saliva forms in my mouth when I envision sizzling hot strips of pork. I reach for the one-pound bag of Starbucks coffee behind a milk jug. A hand warms my shoulder. I jump and spin around. "Mom."

"Beth, I didn't mean to scare you. I heard pots and pans clanging and came down to investigate. What are you doing?"

"Making breakfast. Thought that if I started breakfast now, it would be ready when bedroom alarms go off." Mom yawns and then ambles to the cupboard and reaches for the crackers. "Guess I'm so excited about my find that I couldn't sleep any longer."

No response follows.

Seeing that the woman is totally absorbed with her half-eaten soda cracker, I raise my voice a few decibels. "Are you drinking coffee yet?"

"No, thank you. Still a little nauseated, but I'll try to eat something. The receptionist at Doctor Frank's office penned me in for a four thirty appointment today."

"You still look a little seaweed-green. The color doesn't match your pink robe."

Mom catches my tease and smiles back. "Thanks a lot. Want some help?"

"Sure, that'd be fab."

Mom washes her hands and dries them on a hand towel. "What are you making?"

"Scrambled eggs, bacon, toast, and coffee for Robert if he's still here."

"He's here. I'll microwave the bacon"

Microwave. Microwave. Microwave. I spin back around and grab the bag of coffee.

Mom finishes her thoughts, "And you can scramble the eggs and toast the bread."

"Toasty idea."

"Cute, Beth."

Standing at the counter next to the stove, I add grated medium-sharp cheddar cheese to the eggs, and pop four slices of Dave's Killer Sprouted Wheat Bread into the Toast-R-Oven. When the eggs are scrambled and the bacon is microwaved and the bread is lightly toasted, I yell, "Breakfast's ready."

Moments later, Robert's, Stephanie's, and RC's feet pound the stairs and sound like a herd of elephants. My brother sits on his chair with his eyes half mast, props one elbow on the table, and rests his chin on the open palm. With his other hand, RC jabs eggs with his fork and aims for his mouth but misses the gaping hole because his bent arm holding his head slides off the table. Mom, Robert, Steph and I snicker. With his eyes wide open, his cheeks turn a dark cherry red. He retrieves the egg quickly from the table cloth, stuffs it into his mouth with his fist, and wipes his eyes. Then RC visibly relaxes when Mom and I reach over together and pat him on the back.

After taking care of RC, I'm anxious to meet Jimmy and know his thoughts about the letter, so I dash to the sink, rinse my plate, and slide it into a slot in the dishwasher. Robert walks toward me and tosses his napkin in the wastebasket. "Thanks for breakfast, Beth. The coffee was delicious."

Amazed that he actually stopped to talk to me, I grab the edge of the counter for support. Trying not to show my disbelief, I cock my head and smile. "You're welcome."

RC sings, "The wheels on the bus," on his way up the stairs. Everyone, including me, jumps in. Right now, it feels good to be part of this family. After the song, I—along with my family members—disband and get ready for school and jobs.

❉ ❉ ❉

I hang in the school hallway after geometry and look for Jimmy. When he doesn't come into view, I dial my combination and secure the letter from the suitcase under books. Then get swallowed in the traffic of chattering students as they rush to second period classes. Brian rounds the corner. His shoulders arch like that on a rainbow. He appears deep in thought. My voice flies over the roar. "Hey, Brian."

Brian looks my way and nods and gets behind what resembles a centipede line of students. Then he turns abruptly and marches to his locker. I catch up. He dials the combination, collects music books, and slams the door. It bounces back. He throws it again. It clicks angrily.

I say, "Missed you at practice. What's going on? Are you struggling with a piece for the jazz recital?"

After adjusting his gold-rimmed spectacles, Brian says, "Wasn't at school on Friday because Dad had to go to work, and Mom needed me. She's been throwing up, getting dizzy, and complaining of severe back pain for four days. She thinks it's the flu, but Dad got concerned when she couldn't even keep water down Sunday. When I left

46

this morning, Dad was calling the doctor. I'm not coming back to track practice until Mom's better. Depending on what the doc says, I might miss a couple of days of school too. I'll let Coach Forsythe know."

In my mind's eye, I see a warning sign that reads: "Red Alert." Mom will not be able to swallow water next. I think my imagination might be true because she picked at her food this morning. "Let me know what the doc says, Brian."

He leans against the lockers with sad droopy eyes resembling those on a bloodhound. "Okay."

"Have you told anyone else about your mom?"

"You're the first, Beth. I'll tell the rest of the squad at lunch. See ya." He performs a 180 and drags his feet toward his next class, the music room. His fear, contagious.

During science and Spanish, my worries multiply. "What if, Mom?"

When the lunch bell sounds at eleven thirty, like a snail, I inch my way through the cafeteria line, purchase a carton of milk and a Caesar salad, shield my eyes from the glare, and join the squad at our regular table under the shade canopy. Then I throw my backpack underneath the bench and slip onto the vacant spot between Jimmy and Brian.

Jimmy wraps his arm around my waist and gives me a squeeze. "Hi."

After greeting Jimmy, I focus on Brian and remember what he told me in the hallway.

Like a squirrel, Brian gnaws on his PB & J sandwich that looks like it's been run over by a Mack Truck. He swallows. "My mom's very sick. Dad and I are worried."

Jimmy looks up from eating. "Brian, I'll pray for you and your family."

"Thanks."

Susan and Josh extend sympathy's. Molly throws a quick "sorry," then she spins back around to flirt with Josh.

I face Jimmy. "Gotta ask you a question before next period."

"Ask me now, Beth. I'm all ears."

"No. Not here—in the hall."

Molly jerks her head away from Josh, leans across the table, perches her head on her hand, and zeroes in with eyes like a cafeteria cashier. "Beth, what's the secret?"

Still miffed about her judgmental slurs on Saturday, I say. "Maybe I'll tell you later, but right now, I need Jimmy's opinion on something."

Her eyes widen and roll. "Have it your way." She picks an invisible piece of lint off her shirt, examines her split ends, and spins back around to Josh.

Jimmy wraps his arm around my shoulder. "Beth, if you're finished eating, I'll throw the trash away and meet you at your locker."

I push my plastic tray toward him and rest my hand on his. "Okay."

My locker opens just as Jimmy runs up.

He slings his backpack on the floor between his long legs and reaches for the letter that I'm holding. Jimmy studies it. "Where did you get this? This is great."

"When you dropped me off yesterday, I went to the park and found a suitcase under one of the park benches. This letter was attached to the front. What do you think?" I inhale and let it out slowly.

"Wow." His gaze is intent. "It's—it's about love. What's inside the suitcase?"

"Don't know yet. But, out of curiosity, I lifted the lid and felt around inside. There are small, soft and hard, long and short things—and something that feels like a book. I tossed all night curious about the stickers from Italy, the Hawaiian Islands, and England. Is it possible the suitcase holds a plane ticket for me to travel to one of those places I've never been to?"

Jimmy's shoulders rise and fall.

"Anyway, wanted to share the letter with you. Thought you could explain it to me since you have a God connection and all. What does it mean when the writer says that 'it only takes a spark to get a fire going?'"

He winks. "I'll explain it to you after you do what the letter says: examine the contents and think about love. Okay? Where's the suitcase now?"

"Under my bed for safekeeping. I'm going to open it tonight. But in the meantime"—I put forefinger in front of my closed lips. Then I continue, "it's between you and me, okay?"

Jimmy slides his finger across his closed lips mimicking a zipper. "Catch you at practice." He tears off down the hall.

On my way to history, I wonder if the contents will heal my emotional pain.

Chapter 6

An unfamiliar face rotates the blinds to shield the afternoon glare from faces. Grateful for the humming tabletop fan that cools and dries my perspiration, I hurry to my seat and wait for the man to disclose his identity. The lanky middle-aged male walks with a limp and takes what seems like an eternity to walk from the side windows to the front of the class.

"Good afternoon," I'm Mr. Jefferson. I'll be substituting for Mr. Adams, who is out with the flu." I blow out a long breath and totally relax my worries about Mom and Brian's mom because I'm convinced they both have the flu bug. Then I return my attention to the instructor just as he clears his throat and holds up a newspaper clipping. "I have an article from this morning's paper. When I finish reading it aloud, we'll discuss past relations between the United States and Israel and where we stand today."

Questions and answers fly when he finishes reading. Then a heated debate follows. Some for and some against Israel. I don't participate because I'm hopelessly confused about what I believe. It's hard to form an opinion based on one article written by an editor for the city paper. But I've heard Israel is a holy people who are chosen by God to be His treasured possession. I'll learn more about that another day. Time for English.

After I drop onto my seat, Miss King says, "Pass your homework toward the front of the class. Then get out your books and we'll continue our study of *The Great Gatsby* where we left off. Oh, before I forget, your term papers are due on Monday, June 1. I want you to define *success*. When you finish reading the book, pull out Gatsby's beliefs and then state your own. You can use cause and effect. Any questions?"

No hands go up. Only grunts are heard and yawns seen. Miss King removes her glasses, zeroes in on me and says, "Beth."

I don't have a clue what's coming, but I think about telling her to get outta my face. And don't cross-examine or question me ever again in front of the class. Then I relax when she begs, "Will you please read Chapter 6?"

"Yes, I'll be happy to."

After I finish reading, Miss King closes the class period with, "See you tomorrow."

I, along with other classmates, file out.

As I make my way to the girl's locker room, I think about Gatsby and his life. He had one goal, one desire. It got him nowhere. The result: death. How am I supposed to define *success?*

At my locker, I dress then emerge into the sunlight. Molly jumps in front of my face. "So are you ready to share what you didn't want to tell me at lunch?" She pastes a sticky-sweet cotton candy grin across her face.

"No, I'm not ready." I hate feeling superior. "I'll get back to you when I figure things out." Maybe keeping the suitcase a secret is not such a good idea to our already wounded relationship. I push past Molly.

Coach Forsythe picks up his blue megaphone and calls the squad to join him. I stand in front of the coach. He says, "Hope you're ready for the meet on Saturday. This week we are going to practice hard with a light run on Friday." He swallows. "Susan and Molly, go meet with Coach Stevenson."

Susan waves. "Catch you later, Beth."

Molly scowls at me and then hurries toward her coach.

Coach Forsythe writes something then he looks up. "Josh, Jimmy, and Beth, begin today's practice by returning to the bleachers for your step running exercises. Start with high knees and then skip steps and increase your speed. Do this for forty-five minutes, stretch, and then finish up with a jog of two miles. Don't forget to cool down and stretch again."

I turn toward the bleachers and prepare to take off. Coach stops me. "Beth, looks like you're physically ready for Saturday."

"Yeah. I am. Hope to come in first or second. Want to beat the time of 10.08.11 for my 3,200-meter run."

"Good plan. But I have two things to help you get mentally prepared for your races. The first: run with perseverance the race marked out for you. And, the second: always have a goal in mind."

"Thanks for the info, Coach." I wave and mumble under my breath as I run off. "I have two goals: to solve the mystery behind the suitcase and run my races well. Was the coach thinking about something else?"

❋ ❋ ❋

After practice, I see Mom at the kitchen table thumbing through a *Woman's World* magazine and humming lyrics from her favorite David Foster CD. I tiptoe up behind her and throw my hands over her eyes. I try to mimic Robert's baritone voice, "Guess who? Dinner almost ready?" I plant a kiss on her rosy cheek and step to her side.

Mom finishes a laugh. "Yes."

"What are we having?"

"Chicken, potatoes, carrots, and salad. Sound good?"

I drop my backpack in the hall then return to the kitchen to wash my hands. "Fabulous! You cooking again?"

"Yes."

"You look better than you did this morning, Mom. Glad you got over the flu bug and are back to eating. I was getting worried." I dry my hands on a blue hand towel. "Brian's concerned about his mom. Today, he told me she's been throwing up. But after seeing you now I'll tell him that his anxiety is wasted, worthless." I toss the towel on the counter. "It was fun cooking together this morning. Let's do it again."

"We will. How about right now?" Mom hums to another David Foster selection playing now and dances over to the Crock-Pot on the counter, lifts the lid, and stirs. Smells better than those hot greasy ones at Colonel Sanders's muggy kitchen float through the air. Mom replaces the top, skates over to the refrigerator, opens the door, and hands me a premixed salad pouch with a smile bigger than her ordinary cheek to cheek.

I look at Mom with raised eyebrows, wondering about her strange behavior as I dump lettuce into a green Tupperware bowl. While pinching off brown spots, I ask, "What did the doctor say or do to help you recover so fast from the flu? And why are you acting so weird?"

"He said I don't have the flu." Mom sits on the stool and looks at me with her cheeks glowing like red Christmas bulbs. "I'm acting out of the ordinary because I'm thrilled about being pregnant."

I shove the bowl aside and slap the counter. "You're what?"

Still blushing, Mom repeats, "I'm pregnant. It was a total surprise when Dr. Frank told me today. It wasn't planned." She reaches for a piece of shredded lettuce and nibbles on it like Bugs Bunny. "I can't wait to have another baby."

Still in shock, I say, "Mom, I can't believe you'd do this to me. You have trouble taking care of the kids you've got."

Mom stands and slaps a hand on a hip. "What do you mean, Beth?"

"I've had to fix dinner, take the kids to school, and drive Steph to ballet. What brand of diapers will you be using? Nanny's need to know that kinda stuff?"

"Beth, watch your mouth."

"Sorry, Mom, but those are my feelings." I slide my back down the front of the cupboards, sit cross-legged on the wood floor, and cover my face with my hands, blubbering.

Mom joins me on the floor. "Beth, I love you. I've said it recently and over the years. Haven't you been listening? Your father and I wanted you even before you were born. And I love my other two kids."

"Sorry. Yes, I have listened and I know you love me. But you're always busy. I can't remember when we last spent real quality time together. I feel used. Now with this new brat coming, my chances of getting time alone with you—"

"I'm sorry if I made you feel that way, and I apologize for being so busy with work. You are just as important as Steph, RC, and"— she pats her tummy—"this little one." She plants several kisses on the top of my chestnut hair. "Give me a few days. I'll come up with something so you and I can be alone."

Mom and I hug. I've heard that miracles have happened to people, but because of the past history with Mom, I tell myself to not get excited, just yet.

Mom says, "Right now, Beth, call everyone for dinner. I've got some good news to share."

Comfortable with my place on the floor I yell, "Robert, RC, and Steph, dinner's ready."

"I could've done that, Beth," Mom says with a gleam in her eye.

After Mom and I get up from the floor, my cell rings from the pocket of my backpack in the hallway. I rush to answer the call, flip the cover of the phone, and read the lit words "Saint Joseph Medical Center." I scream, "Hospital!" I rush over and show Mom the highlighted words. Her brows scrunch together. My heart races as I hurry up the stairs to my room. "Hello."

"Beth, it's Brian."

My bedroom door slams behind me. I rush toward the bed and sit on the soft comforter. "Didn't know it was you because I read 'Saint Joseph—'"

He interrupts. "Mom's in the hospital. Dad and I are waiting for the results of the MRI. Mom's sleeping. Unless things turn for the worst, I'll be at school in the morning and I'll fill you and the squad in. Gotta go."

A buzz fills the airways. *Maybe the doctor misdiagnosed Mom. Could she be experiencing a possible high before she crashes and ends up like Brian's mom?* Tears leak from my eyes and spill over the edge.

Steph opens the door and stands in the doorway with one hand on the door jam and the other on the knob. "Mom wants to know what's happening. Your eyes are red."

"Good observation. Tell her to put my dinner in the fridge. I'm not hungry."

Chapter 7

I dry my eyes. Then with a need to concentrate on something other than Mom's pregnancy and Brian's mom's emergency, I get off the bed, lie on the floor, and stretch my arms for the blue-gray suitcase protected in the shadows of the bed skirt and hope there's something in it that will answer my unresolved questions. With the suitcase in hand, I get up and lift it onto my bed. Then scoot with my back against the yellow oversize pillow, drag the comforter over and around my legs, place the suitcase on top of the quilt, and unsnap the latch.

My fingers curl around a small hard object. I draw it into the light and wonder aloud. "What does an antique wall phone have to do with me?"

The front piece of the phone falls off and reveals a pencil sharpener. I immediately think how much Alexander Graham Bell would be blown away at the advancement in communication technology today. My mind races to the words in the letter: let love take you everywhere you go and through each situation. What does love have to do with a pencil sharpener phone? Not liking to feel brainless, I look forward to the next item with a dream that it will expose the reason for the mysterious phone.

Anxiety races through my veins when I reach in and untie a yellow bow around two letters. I turn the first very simple note over. The birthday postcard reads:

November 28, 1909

To the mother of Hugh Mock.

Dear Friend, the name of your little one is on the cradle list of the Wickersham Sunday

55

school primary class. Because it is his birthday, I'm sending this card to let you know that your child is remembered. I pray God will bless you as you strive to train your child for His service.

Very sincerely yours,
Mrs. W. F. Royer, Superintendent

It seems weird to be holding a note that was written 105 years ago. What happened to the child? I wonder if the person married and had a child. If so, the child could be alive today. Why did the card come to me? I don't have a child enrolled in Sunday school. It's not my birthday. Who was the mother supposed to raise her child for? Now more than confused, I move on to what appears to be a more detailed letter.

On the front of the note, three tulips dusted in light magenta stand erect in a clay pot. A butterfly spreads its colorful wings off to the left of the flowers. A silver band frames the scene. I lift the flap. The date: November 5, 1908. It reads:

Dear Harriet. I want to thank you for the afternoon tea you held in honor of my birthday. You are so thoughtful and such a dear. Also, I seek your forgiveness about how I went on and on about Clayton and I being able to purchase our first automobile. I was so excited about the upcoming Sunday drives in the country that I didn't even consider the hard times you have been through. It must have been difficult for you to love me through my boasting. You were so gracious, Harriet. I love you. We have been friends for such a long time. I would do nothing to destroy our friendship.

Love,
Eleanor.

After reading the letter, I sigh because my friendship with Molly continues to wear away, and I don't know how to keep it from total disaster. I choke back tears and groan. Then I think about love and communication, things that I know little about and have no control over. Annoyed with myself for not grasping the hidden messages, I choose to focus on my friendship with Jimmy and promise to come back to the suitcase later.

Tuesday morning, Jimmy waves as I drive into the student lot and park. He stands on the freshly mowed spring grass in his khaki shorts and baby blue shirt. He lowers his shades when I rush up. "Hey, Jimmy."

"Hey, Beth."

I walk in comfortable silence with Jimmy toward classrooms.

With no advanced warning, Jimmy stops and faces me. "Tomorrow night, the youth group is gathering for a serious game of volleyball before the service. Would you be interested?" His Adam's apple goes down hard; his eyes widen to the size of a small doughboy pool.

Rats, I was waiting for the dance question. "Yes. I'll go with you."

"I know you will have fun. Then if you're not sick of me after tomorrow night, would you be my date for the junior-senior prom?"

I throw my arms around his neck. "Yes! Yes! I'll go with you." I stand back, feeling red-faced and wondering if peers, including Molly, see my emotional euphoria and draw unfounded conclusions.

"Jimmy must've seen my discomfort because he draws me in for a comforting hug.

I move away. "Thank you, thank you for asking me. I'm so excited."

The school bell hammers. Jimmy and I say in unison, "See ya."

Jimmy runs off to his first period class. I spot a note taped to the geometry door. It reads: "Teacher out ill. Go to the library."

In the library, with books open and one elbow bent, I rest my head on the open palm and realize what I wanted—a date with Jimmy is *really, truly* going to happen. I'm over the moon exited. Deliriously ecstatic. After an hour of daydreaming, I thread my way through the tangle of students in the hallway. Susan rushes up. "Hey, girl. What's happening?"

"Tell you in a minute." I follow her into the earth science lab, dying to share my fabulous, amazing news. In the back of the room, I sit in front of her and twist halfway around. "Jimmy just asked me to the prom."

"That's great. Jimmy's such a great guy." Susan gives me a thumbs-up and blows a brown curl from her face. Then after a sigh, she says, "I'm going with Todd Wheeler."

"Susan, you and Todd have been dating for a while. Isn't that a good thing?"

"Sometimes I wonder why I'm still with him. Todd says he likes to take me to dances because I'm a good dancer, but between dances I catch him flirting with girls on the sidelines." Susan sighs again. "It's hard to find perfection."

After Susan adds the last syllable to perfection, Todd's six-foot-eight-inch frame draws my attention away from Susan when he runs into the room wearing his black leather jacket. He slides onto a seat in the front row and wheels around and winks. His demeanor displays a pompous "I'm here" attitude. *He's so different from Jimmy.*

Not caring if he sees my eyes roll, I turn back to Susan. "Susan, when you and I ran last week, I thought you had no probs. In a weird way, it's comforting to know that I'm not the only one who is trying to figure things out. We'll talk—"

"Okay—"

A fire alarm squeals and interrupts Susan's further words. My classmates fill the room with chatter. The teacher raps on her desk. When all eyes are on her, she instructs everyone to exit calmly and head for the football field.

After Susan and I gather with the rest of the class on the field, the hook-and-ladder fire truck and ambulance enter the parking lot. Black smoke hovers like an umbrella over the campus. Flames shaped like fingers reach for the sky. Emergency personnel rush toward the music building.

I hyperventilate and wonder about Brian's mom's condition. If it didn't turn for the worst, he promised to be at school today. His second period class is in the music building. Did he make it out alive?

Chapter 8

B lack smoke evaporates after an hour. Fire personnel gather hoses. The ambulance exits the parking lot in silence. *Is there someone in the vehicle dead?* The teacher tells everyone to go home for the rest of the day.

I run to my car and jump in behind the wheel and text Brian, "R U alive," hoping to get a response.

"Yes. Thx. Ltr."

I blow out an audible sigh of relief and start the engine. Police direct school traffic out of the parking lot. When traffic allows, I drive home.

My phone vibrates with Jimmy's music. I scurry up the stairs. "Hey, Jimmy, did you get any further news about the fire?"

"No, but I heard on the radio that all students should watch the noon news for updates about any further school closure.

I plop down on the bedroom floor. "I texted Brian. He's safe."

"Praise God."

The words float around me. What are we supposed to do about track practice today, tomorrow? "When will you pick me up tomorrow?

"Volleyball game starts at six. I'll be on your doorstep at five thirty. I'm sure Coach will call with tomorrow's practice layout and tell us if the school's gonna be closed. Do you want to go for a run in Verdugo Park this afternoon?"

"A run would be good. Could I meet you at the park in about an hour and a half?"

"I'll be looking for you."

"See you later. Bye, Jimmy."

I push End, and hurry down the stairs to the kitchen with the phone still glued to my hand. Totally famished, I dump premixed lettuce greens into a bowl, add crumbled blue cheese and dried cherries.

Next, I throw on walnuts and top it off with a low-calorie balsamic vinaigrette dressing. Needing something to wash it down, I snatch up the last can of Snapple diet peach tea from the fridge and set it on a lunch tray. Pleased with my fixings, I walk into the living room, switch on the TV, and slide onto the overstuffed yellow La-Z-Boy recliner.

Pictures of the charred music building flash across the screen. I chew a large bite of romaine lettuce and concentrate on every word that flows from the newscaster's mouth.

His voice echoes behind the picture of the damaged building. "Fire crews are still mopping up after a fire broke out earlier today at Glendale High. The cause is undetermined. A school official said that the campus will be closed on Wednesday. Classes are set to resume on Thursday."

The reporter announces another component of the news. My cell lights up with the words, "Unknown caller." Because Jimmy said that Coach Forsythe might call, I answer. "Hello."

"Beth, it's Coach Forsythe."

"Thanks for calling, Coach. Jimmy said you might call. Just heard that the school's closed tomorrow. Classes will resume on Thursday. Jimmy and I are going to run this afternoon. What do you want us to work on for today and tomorrow?"

"Glad you are both running today," Coach says. "Begin today and tomorrow's workouts after warming up by doing speed plays. Then move from aerobic walking to anaerobic sprinting. Then do an easy run for five to ten minutes. Follow this with a hard pace for one to two kilometers. Make sure you experience no discomfort before starting the speed work. Intersperse this with sprints of fifty to sixty meters. Continue running until you reach sixty to eighty percent of your maximum heart rate. Don't forget to cool down and stretch. Any questions?"

"Can't think of anything else, but I'm looking forward to the meet on Saturday."

"Good. I know you will race well. Bye."

"Bye." I hang up and get back to lunch.

With the fork in my hand, I open my mouth and take a bite of lettuce and blue cheese. The front door slams. My mother yells, "Beth?"

"Mom, I'm in the living room."

She runs into the room with the speed of a gazelle and digs her high heels into the plush carpet. Unedited questions fly. "Home? Matter? Sick?" Then Mom's warm fingers stretch across my forehead.

I brush her fingers away. "I don't have a fever. I'm home because there was a fire in the music department. Fire personnel and EMTs from the whole city of Glendale showed up. Fire's out, but no school until Thursday."

Mom's shoulders fall after exhaling. My guess: She's pleased that I'm not bleeding out. I stand and offer her the tray with half of my lunch still on it. "Hungry?"

Mom eyes my salad. "Yes, matter-of-fact, I am. That's why I'm home." She turns the ingredients over with the fork and stabs a clump of blue cheese with a dried cherry. "Yum. Got time for a cup of herbal tea?"

"Not now. Since track practice has been cancelled, I promised Jimmy I'd run with him in the park. Can we talk over tea when I get home?"

"Yes. I'll keep the teakettle water hot."

✳ ✳ ✳

Excited that I finally get time with Mom, I step over the back door threshold a half hour before our usual dinner time. Then I freeze because all four members of my family are seated around the kitchen table. My promised date with Mom resembles a flat tire. "Mom, you set aside time to have a one-on-one time with me. Why are you eating? It's not dinner time yet?"

Mom stands and faces me. "Sorry, sweetie. We'll do it another time. The kids came in from playing, and Robert needed a quick meal before his meeting at the airport tonight." She points to my chair. "Come. Tell us about your day." She sits.

I'm totally annoyed that Robert and kids are first on her list again and exasperated that this is the second promise that Mom's broken to me in less than twenty-four hours. But after a couple of ragged breaths, I elect not to pursue the subject because my mouth might get me in an ocean of trouble. I change the subject, sit and look at Mom. "Jimmy asked me to be his date for the prom Saturday night."

Steph sings, "Jimmy and Beth sitting in a tree—"

RC snickers.

Mom reaches across the table for my hand. "Beth, do you have a dress to wear?"

"Well, I do have the blue one that I wore to last year's dance, but I've always had my heart set on a lavender dress."

"Would you like me to take you shopping?"

Filled with static electricity, I jump out of my seat, come to her side, and throw my arms around her neck. "Yes. Mom, you're the best." I return to my chair. "When?"

Mom rises, runs over to the calendar on the wall, retrieves a pen from the junk drawer, and taps the point on what I imagine is a blank square representing an available day. "I could take you tomorrow after work."

"Could we make it another day, Mom? Jimmy's taking me to church tomorrow night for a game of volleyball with the youth group." A spoonful of Dinty Moore beef stew waits on my spoon to be eaten. "Would it be okay if I go?"

"Sure, go ahead. What about shopping on Thursday?"

I chew and swallow a large mouthful of the stew. "Poppins, perfect."

In her nylon stocking feet, Mom skates back to the table with her lips upturned and sits. Then she lovingly lays her hand on Robert's arm and waits for his blue eyes to meet hers. "Honey, could you be here Thursday afternoon to take care of the kids from six until the mall closes? There's lasagna from Costco in the freezer."

I choke. Then pat myself on my back. "Dinner too?"

Robert sits back in his chair. "I could do that." Instead of his usual boring deep facial expression that hardly ever cracks a smile, he gives Mom an affirming nod. Then he throws a wink my way. *How am I supposed to figure this guy out?*

"Thank you, thank you, Mom and Robert." I blow out a breath. "Mom, will you be able to take me to the meet in Mission Viejo this Saturday morning?"

"Yes. The kids and I wouldn't miss it."

Robert raises his hand. "Me too. Don't have to fly out of town until next Monday."

Maybe we can change our names to The Brady Bunch. "Mom, need help with the dishes?"

"Sure."

I help Mom clean up and spend a few hours on homework. Then, too excited to sleep, I think about Jimmy, the volleyball game tomorrow night, the date with Mom to get my gown, and the suitcase.

Anxious to see the next item, I undo the suitcase's latch, open it a crack, and slip my hand in. The setting sun casts an orange glow through the window. It brightens the colors of a small stuffed bear as it unfolds from the depths of the traveling box. His fur is chenille fabric in the colors of a rainbow. A rose-colored bow decorates the neck and shows signs of a water stain. Were they tears of joy or pain from the previous owner or owners? Bet he received a lot of hugs. I hold him up and stare into his penetrating sad-looking, black button eyes. Feeling silly, I ask aloud, "What's on your mind? How did you get four patches?"

Three of the four bear's patches are threadbare scenes of daisies, sunflowers, and twigs—pretty but boring. However, the fourth patch is red-stripped satin in the shape of a heart. It rests over the middle of the bear's chest. It appears new, like it was just stitched on Sunday, the day I picked up the suitcase. My arms prickle with goose bumps. Shivers race down my spine.

Chapter 9

With goose bumps gone for now Jimmy and I arrive at church for a game of volleyball Wednesday evening. He opens the gym door for me. Carol rushes up and stands in front of Jimmy batting her aquamarine eyes. "Hi, Jimmy." I don't remember her as an in-your-face kinda girl.

Jimmy performs like the perfect gentleman, giving her full attention. "Hi, Carol." Then he reaches for my hand and leads me past her.

Carol catches up. "Beth, I'm glad you came tonight."

I hope she's not interested in Jimmy but will show she cares about me.

Jimmy, Carol, and I stand against the wall in the gymnasium and wait for others to show up. Seconds later, guys file in. Jimmy faces everyone. "Tonight's game will be guys against girls. As the team captain I need to get the men organized." He summons the guys to follow him. They huddle.

More girls enter the gym and congregate. Carol faces me; her eyes circle the room like she's trying to find words. "Did you go to another church before you came here?"

I stare at the light brown beechwood floor and twist a strand of hair around and through my fingers. Even though Carol and I had classes together in the past, I never got to know her. Maybe it was because her verbal and nonverbal actions were hard to figure out. At this moment, even though she's a bit straightforward, I answer. "Well, yes and no. Long time ago but haven't been for years because I never understood the Jesus thing."

"Want me to explain?"

"Go for it."

With the energy of a wound up toy, Carol says. "Jesus told everyone that He is the Son of God, but unbelievers accused Him of lying

65

because they thought of Him only as a man. They brought Jesus to Pilate, a Roman governor, who had Him whipped with leather strips that contained pieces of metal and bone."

"I can't imagine the physical pain," I say.

"From the pictures that I saw in *The Passion of the Christ*, the scenes of the lashings to Jesus's body were beyond gruesome." Carol swallows and wipes away a falling tear. "After the sinless Jesus endured the cruel beatings for you and me, they crucified Him."

"Why did He allow them to do that to Him if He is the Son of God?"

"Because of His love for you and me. Jesus suffered on the cross, bled, died, and rose from the grave for all our sins like bad thoughts, hate, jealousy, lying, selfishness, and grumbling."

I saw off a hangnail. "Do you do those things?"

"Yes, and I feel bad about it. After I commit the sin, I run to Jesus in prayer with confession and repentance on my lips. He forgives and—"

Matthew's yell telling the girls to prepare for battle interrupts Carol's next words.

Carol, the girls team captain, dashes off to meet Jimmy for a game of rock paper scissors to see who gets the ball first. Soprano squeals reach the rafters when Carol wins the hand game. I take my place in the front row. Carol slams the ball; it flies over the net.

Guys yell, "I've got it! No, I've got it." The ball lands on the court between Matthew and Nate.

A girl snickers. "One point for us."

Captain Jimmy says, "Okay, guys, let's not let that happen again."

The game ends twenty five to twenty guys.

Sarah pats me on the back. "Beth, you made some great shots. We will win next Wednesday night's game."

Warm bubbles swallow me up and leave me feeling contented like after devouring a meal. Jimmy flies around the net and wraps a long arm around my neck. "Beth, you're not only a great friend but a great player too. Let's go to the service."

On the way to the sanctuary, Jimmy's face adopts deep concentration lines. He pivots on his toes and looks at the group following. "We need to pray for a friend of Beth's and mine. Brian's mom is sick." I join the group as they form a circle. Everyone, including me, bows their heads. Not knowing what to say, I remain quiet when they throw up prayers. After a moment of silence, Jimmy adds, "Amen."

I open my eyes and see Carol standing next to me, opposite Jimmy. "Beth, need to ask you a question."

Jimmy walks on.

"Are you and Jimmy dating? Has he asked you to the prom?"

"Well, we've been seeing each other. I don't know about dating, exactly, but yes, he invited me to the dance, I'm excited." My eyebrows arch. "Why?"

She blushes. "Just wondered. He's so cute, and I don't have a date yet."

If Bma was here, I'd want her to pray and ask God to get her a date. But since my grandma's not here, before I spin around and rush to catch up with Jimmy, I throw parting words to Carol. "I'm sure you'll end up with something, someone."

In the sanctuary, Jimmy and I inch our way into a row that's occupied with Matthew and Sarah. Carol shows up and worms her way in and sits next to me, smiling.

The small orchestra begins playing. Mr. Holland, the music minister, motions for everyone to stand. He says, "Please join me and sing 'Great Is Thy Faithfulness.'"

I search for a hymnbook. Jimmy bumps my shoulder and points to the words on the screen, winking. I inch closer to him, hoping that Carol catches a glimpse.

Following the song, Pastor Rosenburg approaches the podium. "I love God's Word. Don't you?"

A few "yesses" and "amens" come from the congregation as everyone settles on their pews.

With the worshipers settled, the pastor rubs his white mustache. "Okay, I'm glad you're awake. Stay with me now." Pause. "A few days ago, I got permission to share a story about a couple who came in for counseling. The husband said, 'Pastor, my wife and I fight about issues that are about everyday occurrences.'

"I asked, 'Is there a particular issue you're talking about?'

"The husband—we'll call him John—said, 'Yes, but it's a foolish question. We want to know who's responsible for making the coffee in the morning."

Pastor Rosenburg swallows a drink of water from his glass on the pulpit. After the swallow, he continues, "I was a little puzzled at first, but I know God is faithful and is right there when we need Him. I flipped pages of my Bible until I read the word Hebrews. I laughed aloud.

"'What's so funny, Pastor?' The husband, John, asked.

"There are no silly questions because God has an answer for everything we ask. He provided the answer. The answer is 'Hebrews.' You are supposed to make the coffee in the morning, John. A moment of silence passed. When John and his wife understood completely, all three of us laughed in unison. I told John, 'Now you can take care of your wife and make the morning coffee.'"

Jimmy eyeballs me and grins. I think about Steph's song this morning, *First comes love…*

The pastor loudly clears his throat and continues. "The point of the story—God cares about every detail of our lives, even things that we think are silly."

A quiet moment follows. "My sermon for this evening is 'Listening and Doing.' Open your Bibles to the first chapter of James. For those who are unfamiliar, James is near the back just after Hebrews and before 1 Peter. I'll begin at verse 19."

I whisper. "Jimmy, I didn't bring my Bible. Will you share?"

"Sure." Jimmy flips to the passage with no trouble.

Pastor puts on his black-framed glasses and reads, "Everyone should be quick to listen, slow to speak, and slow to become angry for man's anger does not bring about the righteous life that God desires." He looks up at the congregation. "God is telling us in this passage that we shouldn't be quick to speak. But when we do speak, we should try to choose your words wisely. I say 'try' because you will never master it, but we should count on Jesus for His help. He's a good listener and wants to be our Teacher.

"Are you wondering about the benefit of listening? Well, when you're quick to listen to others, you'll not be quickly angered. Real communication is difficult. Try to pay attention to each word that comes out of your mouth. Keep striving to learn. We're not in school for only twelve or sixteen years. We're in school for life." He leans across the pulpit. "To whom will you run to for help?"

The service ends with the song "Nearer, My God, to Thee." I follow Jimmy out of the sanctuary. The brain matter between my two ears spins like a yo-yo with more questions. *How am I supposed to get close to God?*

Jimmy and I get in the car. He asks after a mile or two, "Why are you so quiet, Beth?"

"Sorry. Thinking about what Carol said about Jesus." From the side, I see one of Jimmy's eyebrows arch. "And the pastor's sermon and the contents that I've removed so far from the suitcase. I feel like I'm supposed to keep brainstorming."

After one of his priceless smiles, Jimmy winks. "Beth, I know you'll figure it out. I'm praying for you big time."

For the next mile or so, Jimmy and I sit in silence. Then we arrive at my house and park on the driveway. Jimmy opens my car door and reaches for my hand. When I have both feet on the doorstep, he runs back to the car. "See you in the morning, Beth." Then he waves as he drives off.

I wave back and close the front door. The pastor's last question, 'Who will you run to for help?' whirls in my head like a tornadic waterspout. Confused, I run up the stairs to my room. Maybe putting my thoughts down in my diary will help to unravel the knots in my brain.

Sitting at my desk, I write:

> Dear Diary, haven't written in a while. Been busy.
> Still having trouble deciphering the meanings of
> the items that I've extracted from the suitcase.
> After the bear was a small red hardwood apple.

> That one has me totally freaked out. Why would
> the giver of the suitcase include something to
> make me hungry? It makes me want to sink my
> teeth in a sweet Red Delicious apple.

I stop writing, massage my fingers, and let my mind reel back to two memories. The first is so visual that I want to reach out and finger the pony's white mane. Mom and I stood hand in hand outside a white vinyl fence at a farm and watched an owner feed an apple to his Shetland pony. Streams of juice splashed to the ground and splattered the man's boots. I loved my mother-daughter moment. The pony wandered off.

The memory fades, and my third grade classroom comes into view. Mrs. Williams, my third grade teacher, stood in front of me as I handed her an apple. She wrapped her hands around the red fruit. "Thank you, Beth. Thank you very much." I sauntered to my seat wondering why she was so excited about a dumb piece of fruit.

At the end of the day, Mrs. Williams pulled up a chair next to me and told me the story of John Chapman, better known as Johnny Appleseed. She said he was an American pioneer nurseryman who unselfishly planted apple seeds so other people could eat the fruit. Then Johnny told everyone he met about Jesus. The teacher clapped her hands. "Jesus can teach you many things."

From my open window, the night air brings a cool breeze into my room and forces me back to the moment. I reach for the apple, pick it up, and turn the item over and over in my fingers, remembering about what Mrs. Williams said so many years ago. Then another sentence of Pastor Rosenburg's sermon races through my mind. "Jesus wants to be your Teacher."

A teacher's supposed to guide, instruct, and train. Coach Forsythe does all of that. I believe he has my best interests in mind. But—if Jesus knows what is best for me, He could be doing a better job. Now double, triple, quadruple confused, I need answers. *God, if You're listening, it felt like You were tapping me on the shoulder after the pastor's sermon on Sunday and tonight. If You want my attention, what do You want me to do?*

Anxious for the answers, I set the apple next to the bear on my dresser; grab my Bible, jump on my bed, and flip pages until I come across the concordance in the back. My finger slides down the page and stops at the word "teaches" with the words "Isa. 48:17" underneath it. What does "Isa." mean?

Under the table of contents, I locate "Isa." and discover that it's the abbreviation for Isaiah. Next, I turn to the book within the Book and find chapter 48 verse 17. It reads: "I am the Lord your God, who teaches you what is best for you, who directs you in the way you should go." I chew on my lower lip and tap on the passage with my index finger. *What the pastor said is true. How come I got no help after Daddy disappeared?*

Not receiving an immediate answer, like usual, I take matters into my own hands again. Beth Paine, Female Agent 007, is ready to crack another case: the meaning behind the apple and teacher. At one in the morning, I turn off the light.

Chapter 10

After a late night, I'm glad that Thursday morning's classes pass in a blur. A half hour before noon, I make my way into the cafeteria. The lump of Red Delicious apples in my backpack hammers my spine. Jimmy waves and points to the vacant space next to him. I drop my backpack on the table and it makes a dull, heavy sound. Everyone's eyes, except Molly's, round, protuberant.

Molly shadows her face with her hand and continues to be occupied in a conversation with Josh. I suspect that she's still bugged that I won't tell her about the secret that I have with Jimmy. I wish she'd get over it and move on like she told me to do. If I tell her my thoughts, she might start a verbal catfight. I quash the idea.

Seconds pass, then Molly turns from Josh. "What have you got in there? What going on?"

"Presents." I unzip the backpack and bring out the apples, placing one in front of Susan, Josh, Molly, Brian, and Jimmy, then sink my teeth into my apple and suck the juice.

Josh gives me a thumbs-up. "Thanks, Beth."

Jimmy takes a bite. "It was sweet of you, Beth. Thanks."

Brian twists the stem around, gives it a tug, then follows it with his eyes as it lands on the ground. "The doc told Dad last night that Mom's suffering from an ectopic pregnancy. It's serious. She's scheduled for surgery tomorrow."

Josh says. "My mom had an ectopic pregnancy. All of us waited nervously through the tests and surgery. The child died."

I think big, big mistake. He could've kept the loss a secret. I worry about Mom again. Uncomfortable silence follows Josh's uncalled-for news. Jimmy faces Brian. "Last night, the youth group prayed for you and your family."

Brian's eyes widen. "Thanks."

Molly throws the apple treat into her brown bag without a word of thanks. Susan says, "Hey, girl. Red Delicious—my favorite."

I turn to Jimmy. "Do you know of any stories about the apple in the Bible? Pastor Rosenburg said last night that Jesus is our Teacher."

The corners of Jimmy's lips turn up. "There are no specific references to the apple in the Bible, but the world has come up with the idea that the fruit on the tree of the knowledge of good and evil in the Garden of Eden is an apple. So I'll tell you the story about the fall of man and use the apple as the symbol for the fruit." Jimmy drinks from his milk carton and swallows. "After God created Adam and Eve, he told them that they were free to eat the fruit of any tree in the Garden of Eden, except the fruit from the tree of knowledge of good and evil. Satan, the deceiver, clothed himself as a serpent and entered the garden. His plan was to lead Adam and Eve astray, away from God."

Susan leans across the table and fixes on Jimmy. "What happened next?"

"Satan asked Eve, 'Did God really say that you must not eat from any tree in the garden?'

"Eve said, 'No. God said that we could eat from any tree in the garden except the fruit from the tree of knowledge of good and evil. If we do that, we will die.'

"'That's a lie,' Satan said sharply. 'You will not die. Take a bite you'll see.'

"Eve ignored God's instruction and believed the serpent. She walked over, picked the reddest one, and took a bite. Then she shared the delicious fruit with her husband, Adam. The couple didn't physically die, but when God found them in the garden, everything changed. As soon as Adam and Eve sinned against God by eating fruit from the tree, the process of death began. The couple became susceptible to the physical degeneration of old age and disease and Adam and Eve faced a more serious form of death: spiritual death and eternal separation from God.

"The garden had been a place of perfection, a place where they could connect with God. But after their disobedience, it became a place of shame and fear. God banished them from the Garden of

Eden because they had chosen to walk away from God and do their own thing. That's how sin entered the world. It was the beginning of man's fall."

After finishing the Bible story, Jimmy catches the eyes of Brian, Susan, and me. "Any questions?"

I interrupt the moment of silence. "How is Jesus the Teacher?"

"I'll get back to you when I think you're ready. It will take a while to explain because—"

The bell rings and interrupts Jimmy, signifying that lunch is over. Time for more classes. Molly slings her backpack over a shoulder and lifts her legs over the bench. "I'm leaving because it's getting stuffy here with all this Bible stuff." On her way out of the sunlight, with trash in hand, she aims for the circular file and grumbles loudly after missing the container. Then Molly runs into a dark hallway and disappears.

※ ※ ※

After Molly's hasty retreat from the lunch table, I run like a mouse to cheese toward the eight-hundred finish line at track practice. I catch my breath, shake my legs, and jog in place. Coach approaches. "Good job, Beth. Your time is 2:12.18. Cut four seconds off and you'll beat everyone on Saturday. Run the 3,200 next and I'll meet you at the finish line."

Molly pops up and taps me on the shoulder. "Good job." Then not lingering for more than a nanosecond, she turns and runs back to her coach. I knock my head with my knuckles and attempt to understand her actions. She changes from Dr. Jekyll to Mr. Hyde faster than a chameleon switches color. I don't like the bumpy road. It's annoying and confusing.

Jimmy trots over. "Are you going to run the 3,200 next?"

"That's the plan."

"Would you like a partner?"

"Always. Jimmy, you don't know how much your companionship means to me. Molly"—a tear slips down my cheek.

74

Jimmy stops walking and faces me. "I know Molly is…arrogant. I'm praying for her. Don't let her ruin your goals for Saturday. Come on, pretty girl, you've got work to do so you can win the race this coming weekend."

Motivated by Jimmy's encouraging words, Jimmy and I start off. The bleachers grow less visible, voices fade, and cars on the street in the distance resemble colorful splashes on an artist's canvas. I focus on the track before me and keep my long legs under me. Breathing—in, out, in, out.

Jimmy whizzes past and yells back. "Keep it up, Beth. You look good."

I yell, "Go, Jimmy."

I cross the finish line, bend over, rest my hands on my knees, and catch my breath. "What was my time, Coach?"

"I'm not going to tell you. I've done my best to encourage you. It is my hope that you will inspire the rest of your teammates to keep striving for excellence." He adjusts his cap. "Now, go for an easy five-mile cooldown. You can be dismissed after you've stretched." Then, while folding his clipboard, he adds, "Tomorrow, you can do an easy run on you own. I'll see you at the meet on Saturday."

I jog in place and face Jimmy, who stands next to me. "As soon as I get home, Mom and I are going shopping to buy my dress for the dance. Can't wait."

❄ ❄ ❄

I step into the entry. "Mom? Mom, where are you? I'm ready to go shopping."

"In the living room, Beth."

I see her half asleep on the couch. "Are you sick?" Joy and excitement instantly drain from my heart. "We're supposed to go shopping. You promised."

Mom sits up. "I know I did, sweetie, but Robert's airline added another flight to Florida in preparation for spring break. He received a call about two hours ago. I've got to stay here with Steph and RC—or we could take them with us."

75

"Mom, this was supposed to be our time. Don't want the brats tagging along."

"It's out of my control." Mom reaches for her purse on the footstool, pulls out bills, and presents them to me like a chef holding a silver tray loaded with mouthwatering pastries. "Why don't you call one of your friends to take my place?" She scratches her brow. "I'll think of something we can do together without the kids another day."

Why doesn't she call one of her friends to watch the kids now? Guess it's a matter of priorities. "This was our day, Mom. I'm not going to trust you anymore. This is the third promise you have broken."

Totally depressed and speechless, I glare at Mom, grab the money, and trudge up the stairs to my room. After slamming the door, I kick a pair of shoes out of my path, hug Daddy's picture, and wrap myself in the comforter. Water rushes from my eyes. "I need a Daddy hug." More tears flow when I hold the picture in front of my eyes. "When you were here, life was perfect. You and I did things. Mom and I did things together."

I wipe another tear. My cell buzzes. Susan's number lights up. I sniffle. "Hi, Susan."

"Beth, was wondering how English class went today. Did Molly ever thank you for the apple?"

"No. Shouldn't be surprised. Gave her a ride to school this morning. She didn't thank me before she emerged quickly from the car. She's turning into a mental case. Guess it's time to move on. But it's hard." I sniff again.

Susan asks, "Are you getting a cold?"

"No, just bent out of shape. Mom was going to take me shopping for a prom dress, but now has other plans. Would you go with me?"

Susan laughs. "So am I second on your list?"

"Yeah, but in a good sort of way. If you go with me, I know we'll have a blast. Should've thought of you first. Got money for dinner. Please say you'll go."

"Yes, Beth. Come get me. I'll be waiting by the curb."

Grateful for Susan, I grab my purse and rush down the stairs with the phone glued to my ear. "I'm on my way. See you in a few." I snap the phone shut, open and slam the front door, wondering if Mom knows how upset I am. Then I jump in my car. The wheels screech on my way out of the driveway. Hope there is no police around.

Susan waves as I approach her curb and pull up beside her. She says through my open window, "Hey, girl. You weren't kidding when you said you'd be here in a flash." She jumps in and snaps her seat belt.

"Had to get out of the house. Those kids keep getting in the way." I gulp. "Normally, it takes a long time to get me upset, but with Mom failing to keep promises and Molly's attitude—"

"Understand. It's okay," Susan rechecks her seat belt.

After eyeballing her recheck, I slow down to the speed limit by lightly tapping the break and making sure the gauge reads twenty five until I'm out of the residential area. When we reach the Galleria shopping mall, we're laughing. Susan points to a parking space. Then she and I skip like school children and head for the entrance.

After an hour of zipping through Kohl's, Penneys, Nordstrom, and Windsor with Susan at my heels, I rest my arm on a cold metal rack and gnaw on a nail, totally discouraged after not finding anything to make us happy.

Susan plops onto the nearest chair and wrinkles her face. "Not good, huh?"

"No, but are we quitters?"

Susan stands. "Where to next, fearless leader?"

"Macy's. They'll have our dresses. I'm not giving up until I get the gown that I've dreamed about all my life."

Susan giggles. Then she and I jump on the escalator and ride up to Macy's second floor. Susan dashes down one aisle. Then I see a mannequin dressed in what I envisioned my dress to be, I gasp and run over to get a closer look. The lavender gown is sleeveless and floor length. It has a perfect round neckline, a purple satin ribbon around the waist, and a bow in the back.

My friend comes around the corner holding up a blue satin dress. She proudly caresses the sequins. "What do you think?"

"You'll look so beautiful. Todd won't even notice anyone else in the room." I point to the mannequin.

"It's so you, Beth. Wish I could see Jimmy's reaction when he sees you floating down your stairs. Let's find the dressing rooms."

Susan and I come out in bare feet with our gowns gently tracing our figures. I dance in front of the mirror pretending to be Miss America.

After buying the dresses, Susan and I stuff our faces with pepperoni pizza. Then I drop her off in front of her house. "Thanks for shopping. See you in the morning."

Chapter 11

I pull onto my driveway and switch off the engine. Then hurry to the front door. With the hook of the hanger that holds my dress balancing on the index finger of my left hand, I slip the key into the lock with my right hand and twist it. Then step into the entry. Mom stands with an armload of kids clothes. "Beth, your dress is lovely."

"Thanks." I push past her.

I fly up the stairs to my room and hang the gown in the closet. Then punch in Molly's number and sit on the floor between piles of clothes.

Molly answers on the sixth ring. "What do you want?"

"Did you get a dress for the prom?"

"Beth, you don't really care. What is this call about anyway?"

I chew off a jagged edge on my nail and watch it fly from my lips to the wastebasket. "I wanted you to know that Jimmy asked me to the prom. I found my lavender gown, and it's so perfect."

Molly hangs up.

I snap my phone shut.

After the disconnect, I mumble aloud. "Oh, well. Whatever. Maybe she'll think before she blurts what she knows little about. I brush aside tears that play follow-the-leader like the child's game down my cheeks and pull out the sixth item. It's a muslin hand towel. The top half of the towel is covered with a homey farm setting. A 1917 calendar covers the bottom half.

In the homey scene, a bowl filled with yellow daisies and a pitcher of milk with two glasses stand on the oak table next to bread and cheese in a wicker basket. Lemonade yellow café curtains decorate the nine-paned window. In the distance, an old brown truck bearing the name Hickury Farms is parked in front of the red barn, the barn doors wide open.

79

The kitchen scene causes my heart to remember the smell of Grandma Bma's homemade oatmeal raisin cookies. I swipe tears and turn my focus to the calendar below.

What was so great about a day or event in 1917? Is there something that's supposed to pertain to me? Maybe there's nothing to decode. Maybe I'm supposed to rearrange my schedule. Nah. Can't. Why is it in the suitcase?

I put the towel next to the other items on the dresser. Maybe I'll dream about the meaning. I turn off the light.

※ ※ ※

Friday morning, I walk into Mr. Max's geometry class and see him glaring at me. I give myself a once-over and toss the backpack beneath my assigned seat and slide onto the cold, plastic chair. Max asks, "Who has registered for the SAT?"

I study the room. One half of the class raises their hands; the other half appears just as perplexed as me.

Mr. Max opens his book. "Okay, for those who have not, I would like to see each of you after class so you can make an appointment for consultation." Pause. "Now turn in your books to chapter 10."

I still don't have a clue what I want to do. Was hoping I could put the issue on hold until my senior year.

Following the bell, Max dismisses the class. "That will be all for today."

The bell doesn't usually bother me, but today, it sounds like *braaawnk*. I step up and get in line behind fellow classmates and hope what feels like a nightmare will be over soon. My turn comes. Mr. Max says, "Beth, are you available any day next week after school?"

"Can't. Got track practice." Absolute truth.

"Okay then. How about before school? I can make your appointment the first one on Monday morning. How's that?"

"Guess." Persistent, isn't he?

Black ink flows from his pen onto a white square on his desk calendar. "I'm writing your name down for seven Monday morning.

We'll have an hour before class to go over your grades and plans for the future."

Oh joy. I pull up my cell calendar and add the appointment under "Get Jimmy's boutonniere" on my to-do list. I sigh and then say, "Okay." Then with the appointment over with, I fling my backpack over one shoulder, escape into the hallway, and skirt around groups of loitering students.

Jimmy comes around the corner and elbows me. "On your way to Phys Ed?"

"You offering to walk with?"

"Yes." Jimmy reaches for my backpack and throws it over the shoulder not holding his own. "Brian just texted me and said his mom is scheduled for a hysterectomy at noon. She should be out of recovery by three. He'll keep us posted."

"Good." I'm glad for a quiet moment because my thoughts about the surgery and possible complications with Mom's condition and death spin faster than a Ferris wheel that's totally out of control.

When we approach the door to my classroom, Jimmy hands me my backpack. His hand stays on the strap. "Did you get a dress? If so, what color is it?"

"Lavender. Hope you like it."

"You'll be gorgeous as usual."

"Thanks."

"A few couples from the youth group want to join us for dinner before the dance. Would that be okay with you?"

"Sure. Can't wait. Thanks for carrying my books. See you at lunch."

※ ※ ※

I head for the vacant spot next to Jimmy at our lunch table. After throwing my legs over the bench, I listen as Jimmy shares the news about Brian's mom with Josh, Molly, and Susan. Josh sighs. "Too bad."

Susan leans in. "Can't imagine what it's like to lose—"

Molly cuts Susan off, blinks her mascara lashes rapidly, and shoots her eyes to and fro. "Today in English, we are going to talk about *The Great Gatsby* and the love affair."

I ask, "How can you be so heartless, Molly? We were talking about Brian and the fact that his mother is having major surgery today. His mom and dad have been married for who knows how long and lost a child. Yet you bring up the infidelity between Daisy and—"

Molly stands. "Beth, let me remind you that Daisy and Gatsby were an item once. And they had problems, but"—she fluffs her hair and sits.

Josh rolls his eyes. "Yeah, Molly, but when Gatsby reappears on the scene, he wants a now-married Daisy back. Not cool. Gatsby and Daisy never married. We were talking about Brian's mom and dad, who love each other and were trying to have a child, not Gatsby and his former lover."

I'm so proud of the guy for standing up to Molly and stating the truth. Jimmy folds his arms. "Molly, let me remind you that the story ends in tragedy. When you're married to someone, you're supposed to remain loyal to death. The Bible stresses—"

I let out a tired breath as Molly interrupts again. "Oh, please, not Bible stuff again. I've heard enough." She picks up her tray and books. "Josh, are you coming?"

Josh waves a simple speechless goodbye.

Looking peeved beyond description, Molly gathers her backpack. Her huff and puff resemble that of the Big Bad Wolf, the menacing predatory antagonist.

Josh has a faraway look in his eyes. I elbow him to get his attention and bring him back to the cafeteria. "Oh, sorry for zoning out," Josh says. "Do you like church, Beth?"

"It's good. I was a little cautious the first Sunday, but after being introduced to the youth group, I felt instantly accepted." I look into Jimmy's eyes for affirmation. Jimmy winks.

"Josh, a few couples from the group are joining Jimmy and me for dinner before the dance tomorrow night. Do you think you could convince Molly to change her mind and be part of the group?"

"Because of Molly's new attitude, there's not a chance. Lately, under my breath, I've been referring to her as Deathwyler instead of Molly Dettwyler. Cause I never know how she's gonna react to anything."

I nod.

He takes a breath. "Don't mention it to Molly, but I'll come to church Sunday."

"Great! Jimmy and I will be looking for you. The service starts at ten at First Baptist in Glendale. Do you know where it is?"

"Yes."

I look to Susan and raise my brows. "You in?"

"I'll think on it."

Josh and Susan gather their trash and split. Jimmy gathers the remains of his lunch and turns his head my way. "Do you want to go for a run today."

"Yeah, but no." I raise my upper lip and point to the black and blue sky. "Because it looks like rain for the first time in whenever, I'm going to run an errand and do laps around the block at home. I need to work on getting mentally prepared for the meet tomorrow."

Chapter 12

Saturday morning, Robert throws the gears into park at Trabuco
Hills High in Mission Viejo. I step from the back seat and dash
over to where the squad has gathered. Echoes of laughter radiate
from the grandstands as Moms, Dads, and wiggling siblings antic-
ipate the day's events. A fresh linen breeze floats through the air
leaving hits of last night's rain. The starting line glistens in the rays
of light that peek between puffy-like cotton clouds and beckons all
racers.

I catch up to the group and slip in between Jimmy and Molly.
Molly moves and edges her way in between Josh and Susan. I bite
my lip and try unsuccessfully to will away a tear. After a sniffle, I face
the coach. A word of caution runs between my ears: *don't let Molly
ruin your day.*

Coach questions the group. "Have you all checked in and
received your numbers?"

I along with all of my teammates mumble, "Yes."

"Okay then. Do your warm-ups and meet me by the concession
stand in thirty minutes."

Just before Molly and Susan run off, Molly turns her head and
throws me a look of superiority. I hate her arrogance, uppitiness. Her
shoulder-length brown hair slaps her in the face as she turns to run.
Now, if my sour stomach would settle, I'll be ready to run.

Jimmy, Josh, and I finish our warm-ups, sprints, strides, and
stretches and then run to stand with Coach. Coach slaps Jimmy on
the shoulder. "You're up in five minutes."

"Hey, Beth, may I pray for us?" Jimmy asks, reaching for my
hand. I nod. "Thank You, Father, for today. Help Beth and me to do
our best. Amen."

After the prayer, Jimmy puts his foot on the starting line. He runs his 3,200 meter race with a time of 8:38.51 and crosses the finish line. Winning with an easy, no-sweat first place.

The track clears. I squeeze my hands into fists, then open and stretch my fingers—a trick Jimmy taught me to release tension. I line up for the girls 3,200 and listen for the gun. It fires. I run past the grandstand and look left and right. I'm pumped when I don't see a runner next to me. I encourage myself, "Run, run, run. You can do it."

Sweat coats my neck and chest and trickles down the side of my face. On the seventh lap just before approaching the finish line, my stomach rumbles; my legs feel like noodles. But I push myself forward toward the finish line, inches away. I give myself an extra push, proud I overcame the Molly problem. In a flash, a girl shoots past me. I come in second with a time of 10:10.05.

Although disappointed about second place, I'm happy because I qualified for prelims. I run over to meet the team. Jimmy congratulates. "Way to go, Beth."

The announcer's voice comes over the speaker system. "Runners, get on your mark for the four-hundred-meter dash."

Molly gets set by putting her toe on the starting block. She easily crosses the finish with a time of 53.98—first place. She looks up at the people in the grandstands, bows and receives loud applauses.

I turn my back and roll my eyes. Susan laughs. I give her thumbs-up as she makes her way toward the starting line for the one-hundred-meter hurdles.

Susan positions herself in her lane. The gun goes off. Her chest rises and falls in quick beats. Susan's ponytail barely swings from side to side, her long legs stretch high over the hurdles, and she crosses the finish line under her expected time. A carnation pink grin curls the sides of her mouth.

I applaud her. "Good job, girl."

Josh stretches and lines up for the 1,600. He crosses the finish line 4:07.72 minutes later.

Next is me. The jitters start again. My pulse pounds in my ears as I fight to quiet my breathing. I try to shake Molly's attitude toward me. I tell myself, loudly. "Get over it. She's just being her normal self these days, totally self-centered."

A queasy feeling still rumbles in the pit of my stomach. I inhale slowly and try to relax. Then I run my hand over 275, the number pinned across my chest, and put my toe on the white line. Before the gun goes off, I accidentally step over the line.

The referee announces, "False start on number 275."

I line up for a second try and wipe my sweaty hands on my shorts. Again, because I'm anxious, I accidentally sprint before the blast of the gun. I get pulled from the race. Then hold my stomach and run toward the bleachers where I squat and puke my guts out for the world to see. I'm mad at myself for letting Molly get to me and discouraged because runners don't do false starts in this kind of race. Now everyone's gonna want to know what happened. If I come up with, "It was all Molly's fault," they'll look and point like I'm a child on the fourth grade playground.

Coach Forsythe approaches. "What happened, Beth?"

I hang my head. "Dunno." I walk toward the car and fall to pieces on the back seat.

Mom leans over the front seat. "What happened in the last race?"

"Don't want to talk about it, okay?" I hope this is not the start of more troubles.

※ ※ ※

Angry with myself for letting Molly get to me during my race, I fly up the stairs at home and head for the shower. Under the shower-head, I'm grateful that I won't have to deal with Molly and convinced that the night is reserved for a memorable time with Jimmy.

After the shower, I'm over the moon excited about my dream date. Hurrying now, I towel dry my hair and gather it into a soft updo with waterfall curls. Next, I apply makeup and run to my room. Then I slip into my gown, slide my feet into pumps, and add pearls to my neckline and ears.

A knock rattles my bedroom door. I open the door a crack. RC says, "Beth, Jimmy's here."

"Thanks, bro. Tell Jimmy that I'll be down in a minute." I close the door and get back to hurrying. After a recheck in the mirror, I gather my dress, blow out a long breath, make my way around the corner, and stop at the top of the stairs. Jimmy stands on the landing with wide eyes.

"You look fantastic. Beth, you're beautiful." His lips stretch into a forever grin.

I float down the stairs. "Thanks. You're looking quite handsome in the black tux."

Jimmy hands me a clear plastic box holding a lavender orchid surrounded with baby's breath.

"Thank you. Thank you." I give him a big hug. "I have something for you too."

Mom stands off to the side. "I'll get it." She hurries to the kitchen, brings back the box holding the boutonniere, and hands it to me.

I remove the small lavender rose from the box. "May I pin it on your lapel?"

"Absolutely."

I love being this close to him. My hands shake at the hope of a first kiss later tonight. Mom pins the corsage on my dress. "Okay, kids, picture time. Stand in front of the artificial ficus tree."

"The tree is gorgeous, Mom. Thanks for decorating it with the flashing white lights."

"You're welcome."

I whisper in her ear. "Sorry about my stinkin' attitude on the way home from the meet. I'll explain later."

Mom kisses my forehead. "Okay. You are forgiven. Go stand with your date for pictures."

Jimmy's hand brushes my back and rests gently on my hip. Yellow balls of light dance before my eyes with every snap of the camera, but I don't care. I feel warm and appreciated.

Mom flashes the last picture. "Thanks, kids. Have fun tonight."

I kiss Mom goodbye, then pivot on my toes and look deeply into Jimmy's blue eyes. "Let's go."

The door latches softly as I make my way to the passenger side of the car.

Jimmy's eyes look heavenward. He points up. "Look, Beth, clouds went away. Stars should be out later."

I giggle. "Thanks. You're wonderful." I slide in on the passenger seat. Thinking that a kiss under the stars would be a dream come true.

Jimmy runs around the hood and then jumps in behind the wheel, stretches over the cushion to the back seat, and hands me a long-stemmed pink rose.

"Why?"

"You told me a long time ago that you like pink roses. Thought tonight would be a good time to show you how much I care about you."

I bring the rose to my nose. The petals tickle my nostrils. "I love it. It has the faint sweet smell of baby powder." I know about baby powder because I've been studying up on how to care for my new sister or brother, in case I'm asked. I inhale again. "You're pretty great too."

A moment of silence slips between us. I jump in with two questions. "Did Brian's mom make it through surgery? Do you know if Carol got a date?"

He looks puzzled at my unexpected questions but answers, "Yes, Brian's mom is in the ICU unit recovering. And yes, James invited Carol to the dance."

My heart skips for joy at the good news because tonight—no problems allowed.

❋ ❋ ❋

After stuffing myself at The Cheesecake Factory, Jimmy and I hurry toward the school gymnasium. Once inside, I draw in a long breath and stand. "Oh, it's beautiful and perfect."

A banner reads, "Junior-Senior Prom Spring Fever," above the stage. Below the sign are pots of pink tulips; yellow daffodils; and bouquets of purple, blue, and white hydrangea. Artificial trees draped with white twinkling Christmas lights dot the dance floor. A disc ball hangs from the ceiling and sends continuous diamonds on the floor and couples.

Jimmy taps me on the shoulder, shaking me from my paralyzed moment of awe. "Do you want to dance?"

"Yes."

He escorts me to the middle of the floor.

"Why are we in the center?"

"Because I want to show you off."

I blush and feel like Cinderella at the ball.

Susan runs up and interrupts our dance. "Beth, you've gotta come with me to the bathroom."

"What's so important?"

"Tell you in a minute. Hurry."

Annoyed at the interruption, Jimmy says, "Susan, we just got here." Jimmy twirls me.

I say, "Yeah. What's so important, Susan?"

Susan jumps up and down like popcorn in a kettle. Then she runs toward the ladies' room and turns to see if I'm following. Then she scoops up the air while mouthing a demand for me to hurry.

My eyes meet Jimmy's. "Would it be okay if I go with her when this dance is over? I'll be right back."

His bright-blue eyes turn to a dull gray. "Looks like I don't have a choice."

The music ends on a low note. Everyone but Jimmy claps. He walks to the sidelines and pours himself a glass of red punch. I run over to Susan. She pulls me into the corner and half-whispers. "Did you see him?"

"Who?"

"Greg, the new addition to the junior class."

"Why should I care, Susan? I've got a perfect date. Why are you so interested? Where's Todd?"

"He went to talk with one of his former girlfriends. Tell me what you think. Greg's totally the biggest and cutest hunk I've seen in the longest time. He's standing near the refreshments. Follow me."

I follow Susan to the refreshment table. The guy spots me looking in his direction and waves. I quickly look away.

Jimmy returns to my side. "What's so important? Beth, you've been gone for a long time."

"Susan wanted to show me the new guy who just joined the junior class. "Come on, Jimmy. Let's dance."

Jimmy rests his hand on my waist. It feels like a wilted flower. Uneasiness, an uninvited guest, steps in the space between us for the rest of the evening.

After the last soundtrack, Jimmy takes quick strides to the parking lot. I'm left to follow if I want a ride home. No time is spent under the stars. He opens the passenger door and heads for the driver's side. Silence sits on the console between Jimmy and me for the entire ride home.

Jimmy drives onto my driveway and shifts the gears to park. The engine idles. His shoulders slouch. Without releasing his grip on the steering wheel, he asks, "Will you be ready at nine thirty?"

Ashamed that I went with Susan and ruined what could have been a dreamy date, tears cloud up and blur my vision. "Sure. Thanks for the rose...everything. Can we talk, Jimmy?"

"Not now." He jumps from the driver's side, opens my door without looking me in the eye, and walks me to the porch. Then Jimmy turns on his heels and doesn't wave back as he throws the car into reverse. Seconds later, the taillights on his car get smaller and smaller.

Fearful that I lost my best friend, I open the front door and stare at the now empty driveway. My eyes drift upward to the black blanket sprinkled with Jimmy's order of stars. He treated me like Cinderella. I wanted him to feel like Prince Charming. *We'll be okay after I talk to him in the morning.*

Sunday morning, contemporary Christian music echoes from the pocket of my backpack on the floor. I rub sleep from my eyes, reach for the phone, and answer. My voice crackles. "Hey, Jimmy."

"I won't be going to church this morning because my grandma had a massive heart attack and died last night. My dad is making reservations to fly to Oregon for the memorial service."

Shocked by the news and the business tone of his voice, I sit up straight. "Is there anything I can do?"

"Well, are you going?"

My words shake. "It was my plan."

"Great. Would you tell the youth group to pray for my dad? This is really hard for him. Gotta go."

"Wait. If I don't make it for some reason, can I have Carol's number so I can give her a heads-up? Can we talk now?"

Jimmy rattles off Carol's number. Then a click follows. I chew off a splintered nail and wonder what my hands will look like when he gets back. I hate his unfriendly attitude. Not in the mood for church, I call Carol.

A recorded voice on Carol's phone answers and instructs the caller: "Sorry I missed your call. Leave a message. God bless and have a great day."

After leaving the prayer request, I slowly lay my cell on the nightstand. How can I have a great day when I've got enough woes to fill a semitruck? A single tear slides down my cheek when the small voice in my head convicts, *You sure made a mess of last night, didn't you, girl?*

I answer aloud, "Yeah, but I'll fix it when Jimmy comes home. Then we'll be good friends again." Then I push my worries aside for now, slide off the bed, and reach for the suitcase under the bed skirt. A memory of a time in Bma's garden comes to mind when I pull out a long-stemmed pink plastic rosebud.

My mind floats back to a day when I was seven. I see myself closing up my crayon box and coloring book and complaining to grandma. "Bma, I'm bored."

She said, "Let's go for a little walk down the garden path. The roses have bloomed."

I walked with her hand in hand on the path. The California sun warmed my back. Bluebirds made their low-pitched tu-a-wee with a complaining tone in the plum tree and the hummingbirds flocked to sugar water. Soft, sweet scents came from the yellow, pink, white, and red roses in the garden below. I dropped grandma's hand and ran. My shoes crushed the long grass.

"Watch out, Beth," Grandma cautioned. "The roses have thorns."

I stopped in front of a small pink rosebush. Bma caught up and gently pulled a single bud toward my nose. "Roses are beautiful flowers, but they need care. It's just like you, Beth. You are like a rosebud now because you are young and tender. God, the Master Gardener, wants to help you grow strong and tall, like the red roses." She pointed to the full-grown bushes. "Let Him take care of you."

Bma smiled. Then she continued, "When I visit the garden, I remember God's love for me."

I followed Bma to the lawn chair and jumped onto her lap. "Beth, the red and pink roses mean similar but different things. Red roses are given on Valentine's Day and anniversaries to express deep love. Relationships are important." She stopped her lesson and whispered, "Beth, I love you."

"Love you too, Bma." I wrapped my tiny arms around her neck.

She continued, "My favorite one is the pink rose because it not only conveys love but also appreciation."

"It will always be my favorite too." I snuggled a little closer to Bma.

Even though the phone rings and jars me back to the present moment, I hold Bma's words in my heart. Then I lay the plastic rose alongside the one that Jimmy gave me and answer my cell.

Chapter 13

"Unknown caller" appears on the screen. It's probably a wrong number, but at this point in my life I don't care. I answer and a cautious hello slips out.

"You don't know me, but I'm Greg Madison. I waved to you at the dance. Did you see?"

My heart races with nervous excitement. I saw an uneven fingernail with my teeth. "How did you get my number?"

"From Todd. You were gorgeous. Were you with someone?"

"Yeah, I was with Jimmy."

"Are you…" His voice trails.

"Jimmy and I are just track friends. Known him since middle school."

"Since you're just friends, will you hang with me today? I've got a Mercedes and and I'll leave the top down. I've never seen the ocean."

I reach for Jimmy's rose and twirl the stem in my fingers. If I went with him, it wouldn't be like I'd be two-timing Jimmy because we've never been declared an item. He'd be proud of me for being kind to someone new to campus. "Maybe. But tell me a few things about yourself, Greg." I pick up a pad and draw a line down to separate two columns. One for good parts and another labeled with a question mark.

"I'll be playing basketball this next season. With me on the team, Glendale High will bring home a trophy. My parents are divorced. My dad works for Marathon Oil Corporation. He flies between Alaska and Texas. He wanted to be centrally located between the two states. My mom lives in Paris, France. I don't have any brothers or sisters. My only restriction…gets good grades. Not bad, huh?"

I listen, making no immediate verbal response. But having second thoughts about this so-called date, I write "possible ego problem" under the second column and retrace the question mark with a red-tip pencil. "You seem pretty satisfied."

"No complaints."

"When do you see your mom?"

"I fly over there, or Mom comes here about once a year. She's busy, but it doesn't matter. I can take care of myself."

"Don't you miss her?"

"No. We hardly talk."

Hmm. My first impression: he's so into himself. Then again, he doesn't seem to be bitter over the detachment of his mother. Not like me who's wallowing in pain over my losses like a pig in the mud. I ask, wanting to know more, "Are you going to college?"

"Yeah. My dad says he'll foot the bill. No idea of a major yet, so maybe I'll find a college and join a fraternity. If I don't make the GPA, Dad will get me in. He's got clout. How about you?"

"Right now, I'm clueless, Greg. I'm sure I'll come up with something."

Silence drifts in like fog, but then it vanishes when he repeats his initial question, "So, Beth, wanna hang out?"

A voice inside my head encourages, *Go ahead. Enjoy. Have a great day. It'll be a new experience. What could it hurt? Give the weird guy a try.*

"Sure, I'll go with you." I write "Could be Fun" in big black bold letters next to the question mark.

"Great. Give me your address. I'll pick you up at eleven."

I glance at the clock; it reads ten thirty. "I live at 2906 Lakeview Terrace Drive. I'll be ready in a half hour." Then I hang up, sit on the bed, and chew off a nail while wondering about Greg. I feel fidgety and excited at the same time.

A minute later, my thoughts make a U-turn to Molly. This will put her over the edge. I'll deal with her another day, if she finds out. I walk over to the closet, push the evening gown aside, and find something to wear to the beach.

Tires screech; a horn honks. I look out my upstairs window. Greg stays in the driver's seat of his red Mercedes-Benz with no attempt to come and knock on my door. I turn my back to the car, wondering about my decision.

But then, dismissing all second thoughts, I zip down the stairs and dash into the kitchen, where I scribble a note to Mom. "Went to the coast." Then I run to the waiting car and stand next to the closed passenger door. Greg grins from ear to ear. "Jump in. Let's go."

"Aren't you going to get out and open the door for me?"

"Can't you open your own door? You look capable."

I swallow angry words before they leave my lips. The voice in my head says, *It's a nice, warm day. Enjoy yourself.*

I make more mental notes, grab the highly polished silver handle, jump in, and fasten my seat belt.

Greg caresses the soft white leather upholstery. "Classy car, huh?"

"Yes."

"It's an SL 65 AMG roadster—top of the line. A V8 engine with 493 horsepower. Impressed?"

"Your car's pretty cool. Looks like you keep it in good shape too."

"Wash it every day." His foot punches the throttle.

My head and shoulders snap back toward the headrest as he rounds the residential corner at well over the speed limit for the housing district. My body jerks toward my locked door. "Be careful. I'm breakable." A song that Bma taught me pops into my head. Even though I know little of its meaning, I've always hummed the tune "Rock of Ages" when I'm afraid.

Greg grins. "Sorry. Which way to the beach?"

"You'll need to get on the freeway."

"Okay." He pushes on the throttle with more power. Tires squeal as he slips and slides around another curve toward the on-ramp.

I scream. "Watch it."

"Relax." He insists over the breeze while increasing his speed. "I've got this baby under control." He looks in the rearview mirror and brushes a dark curl off his forehead. "I thought we'd pick up some burgers when we get there. Okay?"

"Sure, if I'm still alive." Greg rolls his eyes and selects a lane on the freeway. I find myself wondering about church and the topic of today's sermon. "Do you go to church?"

Greg looks at me with a raised brow. "Why would I want to go there?"

"Just a question."

He snaps, "I don't need a crutch. I like being my own boss. Are you into that whole religious thing?"

"Yes. I'm getting into it because I've got a ton of questions and need answers. I went because Jimmy invited me. The kids in the youth group are great and Pastor Rosenburg shares things from the Bible that makes me want to go back and learn more."

Greg turns his head. "Why didn't you go today?"

"Wanted to meet you."

Laughing, he asks, "So I beat out God, eh?"

Sweat collects around my nose and on my forehead when I realize I might have made a serious mistake by not going to church.

Greg continues to laugh, exits Highway 101, and comes to a stop for a red light just before a railroad crossing on Casitas Pass Road. While waiting for the light to change, Greg throws the car into neutral and presses the throttle. His impatience makes me nervous. A couple in the car beside us glare with open mouths. Hoping to distract him, I point to the burger joint called The Spot on the other side of the railroad tracks.

The red light flashes and the guard rails come down. The engineer on the approaching train blows the whistle.

"Hold on. We can beat it." Greg mimics a race car driver. The speedometer goes from zero to fifty when he snakes around the rails. The engineer blows the whistle again. Greg laughs aloud when he makes it to the other side and throws the gears into park at the fast-food restaurant. He stares at me with an excessive feeling of self-satisfaction.

"You scared me. What would've happened if the car stalled?"

Greg rolls his eyes and pats the steering wheel. "Wouldn't happen with this baby. Let's get lunch and take it to the beach."

96

My white knuckles remain glued to the seat cushion. *Be still my stomach.*

The greasy grilled beef fills my nostrils on the short drive to the parking lot of Carpinteria State Beach. The sun casts its light on the ocean and makes flying diamonds out of the spray before landing on the children playing tag with the waves. A small tornado arrives next to the car and tosses sand particles onto my unwrapped burger. "Could you put up the top?"

"Could but won't. It's a beautiful day. Enjoy and eat up."

Disgusted, I wrap the tissue paper around what could have been a tasty burger had sand not jumped in. My stomach grumbles at not being fed.

"Don't like your lunch?"

"Not when it's dotted with beach debris."

Not showing any concern that I still might be hungry, Greg shakes his head while he pushes the rest of the burger into his gaping mouth and removes his shoes. "Let's wade out to the rocks. There might be some sea life caught in the swirls. I'll help you."

I beg, "Let's call it a day."

Greg raises the roof and jumps out. "Not a chance." Then with one hand on the door, he says, "Lock the car by pushing down the buttons. I've got the key." His shoeless feet dig into the sand as he runs toward the water.

Totally miffed, I remove my shoes, run to catch up, and join him on a large boulder. The salt water sprays a fine mist and stings and resembles bites of red ants.

I kneel down and watch the surf brush over purple and red starfish, mussels, sea anemone (which is called the flower of the sea), and urchins. Then I pick up a strand of floating kelp and feed it to the urchins. They draw it in with their mouths. "Pretty cool, huh?"

Greg, appearing bored, shrugs his shoulders and jumps to a larger jagged rock. "Come on. You can make it."

"Give me your hand. If I twist my ankle, my running goals will be crushed for this season."

He throws a disgusted scowl, looks at his watch, leaps back onto my rock, and runs past me toward his precious car. A large swell rushes over me and causes me to slide feet first into the water between the two rocks. The overdose of saltwater sickens me. I come up holding my side and coughing. Then I shake like a drenched dog and make my way to the shore where I find Greg sitting on a piece of driftwood putting on his socks and shoes.

He chuckles. "What happened to you?"

"I fell. You said you'd help. I reached for your hand. Why did you leave me?"

"Gotta get home. Got a date."

I lean in closer. "What?"

"Are you deaf? I've got a date."

My hands slap my hips. "Am I a fill-in for your unscheduled hours?"

He jumps up and brushes himself off. "We need to hurry."

"If you're in the hurry mode, I'm not interested. I know your definition of the word. I'll find my own way home."

"Fine." He sprints toward his prized Mercedes and throws my shoes and backpack with cell phone in it on the sand in front of the car.

Fearful of Mom's response, I rethink the situation and run to catch up. I slap the closed window. "Greg, open up. I wanna talk." He shakes his head, revs the engine, turns the car into a sharp right, and merges with the oncoming traffic. I tie on my tennis shoes and run to the burger joint to call home.

After three rings, RC answers. "Hello."

"RC, it's Beth. Where's Mom?"

"She's in the living room. Where are you?"

"Never mind. Go get Mom. Now."

Mom comes to the phone with anger in each word. "Beth, where are you?"

"I'm on the beach in Carpinteria. I've had an awful day. Come and get me."

"How did you get there?"

"I'll explain later. I'm at The Spot, a burger joint. Come as fast as you can. I'm roasting in this heat."

She sighs loudly. "Okay, I'll be there with the kids. You're in deep trouble."

I wonder about Mom's definition of trouble. *Will I be incarcerated in my room forever?* I'm glad I have enough money from my allowance for a real burger and a Coke. Because it could be my last meal for who knows how long.

※ ※ ※

Mom arrives at The Spot after an hour and a half. She pulls up, rolls down the window, and glares. "Beth, be prepared to explain yourself when we get home. Get in."

The trip home—strained. Stephanie and RC resemble porcelain figurines on the back seat for the entire journey.

At home, Mom pulls onto the driveway. "I'll meet you in your bedroom young lady."

I trudge up the steps to await sentencing. Before leaping on the bed and gathering the comforter around my legs, I grab the Kleenex box. Never imagining that tissues would become one of my closest friends.

Mom walks in, clears a spot on the floor, and sits. "Tell me about this mess you've gotten yourself into." She threatens, "Don't leave anything out."

I pluck a tissue out of the box and squeeze it in my fist. "Well, did you get my note?"

"Yes, but it didn't tell me where you were on the coast or who you were with. I called Jimmy's house, but no one answered. Did you go to church with Jimmy?"

"No. Jimmy couldn't go because his grandma died. He and his family flew to go to services in Oregon." I tear off a nail. "Greg, a new guy in the junior class, called this morning and wanted me to show him the ocean. I agreed to go because it sounded like fun. I didn't have anything better to do. At the time, it felt okay. The day turned out to be as much fun as a root canal."

Mom covers her mouth with a hand. My guess is that she's suppressing a grin. Then she rests against my dresser and pulls her legs to her chest and hugs them. "I thought you liked Jimmy."

"Oh, I do. But Greg seemed interesting and I wanted another friend. He moved here from the Midwest and hadn't seen the ocean yet, so I thought I'd be kind and show him around. I didn't know my curiosity would get me into so much trouble. He's horrible. Today was bad, but it could've turned out worse."

She uncurls herself and narrows the gap between us. "What do you mean?"

"When he stopped for a red light, I saw a train coming. He gunned the engine and made it to the other side of the tracks seconds before the train approached the intersection. With my luck, he'll be in one of my classes next week." A mist covers Mom's blue eyes.

She reaches for the Kleenex box and blows her nose. "Beth, I could've lost you."

I realize at this moment that I'm more important than a live-in babysitter. I slide off my bed, join Mom on the floor, and sob on her shoulder. Moments later, I look into her eyes. "I made a bad choice. I had a problem and didn't know what to do. I felt like a giraffe with a stiff neck. I don't know why I went with him. I sensed his questionable behavior even before I agreed to go with him. Mom, I'll never go out with someone I don't know *ever* again. I am so, so sorry. Will you forgive me for being so stupid?"

Mom rubs my back. "Beth, I forgive you. I'm sorry about your day. I was going to ground you until your first social security check arrived but—"

My eyes widen with disbelief.

"I'll take back the idea"—she winks—"because you're suffering enough from the consequences of your decision."

"Thanks. That's the truth."

"What happened to your head?"

"Lost my balance and fell between two rocks."

"Go put some Neosporin on it." Mom gives me a quick kiss on the cheek, gets up, and turns on the way out. "Take a nap. Dinner will be on the table at six." The door closes quietly behind her.

My cell rings and flashes Carol's number. "Hey, Carol."

"Beth, I got your message and the group prayed for Jimmy and his family this morning. But why didn't you come to today's service? We missed you."

I lie because I don't want to start bawling again over my unintelligent choices. "Mom, wanted to take me shopping."

"One of these days, you'll have to show me what you bought," Carol says.

"Sure. I'm tired."

"Okay, see you Wednesday."

"Bye, Carol."

Chapter 14

I park in the student lot fifteen minutes before my Monday appointment with Mr. Max. When I pick up my backpack, it feels like a hundred pounds of cinder blocks as I sling it over my shoulder. Maybe it's because of the lies I've told. They keep haunting me. I emerge from the driver's side and bump into a body. I spin around. "Susan."

Susan giggles. "Sorry. Didn't mean to scare you."

"Why are you here?"

"Have to do some research in the library. When I saw you, thought we'd walk together. You?"

"Last Friday, Max made me make an appointment to talk about the upcoming SAT."

"How's everything else?"

I tell her the short version about yesterday. "I went out with Greg Madison."

She stops on the blacktop. "No way. You went on a date with the new guy?"

"Quiet. It's not for the whole world to know. He pressured me into showing him the beach. He might be a hunk. But, he's a total jerk. I had to call Mom and ask her to come and get me. She was irritated about having to drive to Carpinteria. Life will be sweeter if I never have to see him again." I blow out a long stream of hot air.

Susan says, "Sorry. Gotta go, but I want to know more. See you at lunch, Beth."

The alarm on my cell goes off, reminding me it's time to meet Mr. Max. I throw Susan a wave and head for geometry.

My hand rests on the door knob. I don't usually have a problem making decisions for the things I want, but the difficulty arises when I don't know what to do. I get very upset when I can't see the solutions, and I abhor pressure. I bite my lip and turn the handle.

Mr. Max turns his head from his throne. "Come in, Beth. Have a seat."

I slide onto a chair and face the teacher.

He announces, "You did very well on your last exam." He holds up my test and hands it to me.

I see an A and say, "Thanks." Then wait impatiently for the question.

"So are you going to sit for the SAT?"

"No."

"Why not? With your grades, you should have no trouble acing the test."

Although surprised by his encouragement, it doesn't stop me from asking, "Do I have to take the test because everyone else in America is taking it? I don't know what I want to do with my life."

Mr. Max bows his head, folds his arms, and stares into my eyes. "I understand."

Unconvinced that he understands, I look off to the side, hoping he will dismiss me. Seconds later, I know that getting discharged is a fat chance because Max picks up where he left off. "Beth, I understand because when I was in high school, I had no idea what I wanted to do with my life. But after peers encouraged me to further my education, I jumped in and viewed college not as an obstacle but as an opportunity. Then during my second year, it became clear to me that I wanted to follow in my father's footsteps and be a teacher.

"If you don't take the test soon, Beth, you'll miss the deadline for applying for the college of your choice or any college. You can take it in your senior year, but the pressure will be greater. I want you to enjoy your last year at Glendale High. I'm trying to help you detour problems. Many colleges require the test scores and applications the first part of November. Do you understand what I'm saying here?"

"Why the meeting today? You said the last day to register isn't until May 5. It's only the twenty-fifth of March. And what's wrong with a junior college?"

"I wanted to meet with you today so that you will start to think about it. With your grades, you have the potential to go far in life.

Beth, there's nothing wrong with a junior college, but the number of degree programs, majors, and class options exceeds what you can get at a typical community college like Glendale Community. And program variation allows one to get more specific in selecting a degree. It has been proven that students who enroll in a four-year college earn more money than those with an AA degree." Max sighs. Then he looks at the desk calendar and taps a pencil. "Are you going to sign up?

Feeling trapped I surrender. "Okay, I'll register."

"Good. I'll see you in class in a half hour."

Still not totally convinced that taking the SAT is right for me, I hightail it out of Geometry 1.

The next two classes zip by then, before I know it, lunch time arrives. With my stomach complaining loudly, I make a beeline for the cafeteria and slide in next to Susan and across from Molly and Josh. "Hey, squad, any new news?"

From Molly, I get no recognition; as usual, she appears captivated in a private conversation with Josh. Susan answers my question. "Nothing much, but where's Jimmy? Brian?"

"Jimmy left Sunday morning to attend his grandma's funeral in Oregon, and Brian's with his mom at the hospital. She was rushed back into surgery with a minor complication."

Molly must've been listening with half an ear to the conversation because she leans across the table and throws a sarcastic question. "So, did ya go to church by yourself?" A snicker follows.

I want to bark at her but catch myself. "No, something came up."

"What?" she asks in her high-and-mighty tone.

Because Molly doesn't talk to me, I see no reason to share details with her. "Went to the coast."

"Oh, but I thought you were into the religious thing." She brushes lint from her purple Ralph Lauren polo shirt and looks up.

I throw her a dirty look and concentrate on a long drink from my ice tea. Thankfully, Susan jumps in as Molly backs off. "Hey, how did it go with Mr. Max this morning?"

"Told him I'd register for the SAT before the deadline of—"

Molly interrupts, "Speaking of deadlines, our English papers are due in a couple of weeks. We're going to have another discussion about *The Great Gatsby* today. When you're finished writing, I'd love to see your paper, Beth."

Her hostile attacks leave me physically and emotionally exhausted. Incapable of knowing what's behind those brown flashy eyes, I don't answer. But if I did, my words would be "when your brown eyes turn blue, which would be never."

I look for an escape. The lunch bell rings. Should I say ah at the perfect timing or yuck because it's time for another possible debate with Molly in English?

Greg waves to me from the seat behind Molly as soon as I slink onto my seat in English. My breaths—short, ragged. Miss King says. "Today is the final class discussion to help you gather thoughts for the term paper. Who wants to open the debate?"

Josh, who sits across from Molly, speaks up. "The affairs between Gatsby and Daisy and Tom and Myrtle plus the romantic relationship between Nick and Jordan lead to a sorrowful ending. The book, a downer."

Molly stands and glares at Josh. "I liked the story because Gatsby does everything he can to win Daisy's heart. Isn't that one way of showing that you love someone?" She lowers herself slowly onto her chair with a sly smile.

Greg says, "I agree with Molly."

Molly turns around and gives him a high five.

Sitting in front of Molly, I spin around with my eyes fastened into her black-brown eyes. "Yes, love is about getting Mr. or Ms. Right but not when the one you want is married. Where did it get Gatsby?"

Molly is red-faced, speechless. If I could see inside her head, I would see her brain screech to a stop like newspaper presses. She knows the result.

Steven, to my left, paints a visual picture of the outcome when he opens his mouth, draws his index finger across his throat, and gasps. His eyes close. His blond head falls on the desk with a very hard *thump*.

Miss King raises an open palm to silence the class' snickers. "Continue, Beth. Sorry for the interruption." Her own amusement at the jokester's skit follows with a laugh.

I choke back a giggle. "Steven's right. Gatsby ended up dead. Nick went home totally disgusted after witnessing greed, hatred, jealousy, and anger. Daisy, although she was shallow, selfish, and hurtful, promised God she would stay married to Tom. Marriage is a partnership and is supposed to last until death."

Satisfied with my decision, I escape mentally and think about last night. After Carol's call, I took Mom's advice and napped. I woke energized and reached for the suitcase. From its mouth, I unfolded a tea-colored muslin cloth with frayed edges and embroidered black words. The words said, "Marriage is a garden gate. Along the path there will be flowers and weeds. Cherish the flowers and pull the weeds."

In the middle of blades of grass stood two tall red daisies. I didn't understand the meaning or the reason for the cloth being put in there for me since I'm only sixteen. If God is watching out for me, I'd tell Him to please cross Greg off your list. Bring Jimmy home. Quick. I scratch an itch. It brings me back to the classroom.

Miss King's words interrupt any further thoughts. "I hope today's discussion helped you to formulate your plans for the assignment. You might want to begin with an outline. Does anyone have any questions or further comments?" No responses follow. "See you tomorrow."

I join the swelling flow of students in the hallway. A poke digs into my shoulder. I spin around.

Greg's lips turn into a Crest toothpaste smile. "Can we talk?"

"Nothing to talk about. You were the one who left me standing on the beach."

He grabs my forearm and pulls me toward a locker bay.

My teeth clinch. "Let go."

"Okay, okay." He releases his hold. "Why am I getting the cold shoulder?" he asks with an open palm on a locker. Then he leans into his straightened arm, looking confused.

Should I feel sorry for his melted brain? "Greg, let me clarify. You're cute, but you need help. Might want to check out the definition of manipulator." His arm falls to his side. "Did you treat your second date on Sunday the same way you treated me?"

For the first time since he pulled up in front of my house in his "baby," he's speechless. Pleased with myself, I escape from Greg, push open the double doors, and exit into the sunlight. Then I head for the girls' locker in Building 5.

Susan runs up. "Want company?"

"Yes. Need it."

"You look like you just fought a bull. What happened? How has your life changed since lunch?"

I scan the grounds. "Hope I knocked some sense into Greg's thick skull when I blurted out my true feeling to him. He's a creep or incredibly dense."

"You've got more nerve than me. Wish I could be more like you."

"Don't be so quick to applaud me. One minute, I think I'm doing something wonderful. Then the next minute I feel like pond scum."

Susan kicks a pebble from our path. "I hope I can be as strong as you when I bring up a few issues with Todd."

Molly yells from an uncomfortable distance. "Beth, wait up. Got news."

"You might have to solve another problem, Beth." Susan's face sympathetic, she runs past Molly.

Molly stands in front of me with one hand on a hip. I wonder who is going to speak. Will it be the criminal mastermind Mr. Hyde or the kind, respected English doctor Dr. Jekyll?

"You didn't tell me you went out with Greg Madison on Sunday, Beth." She inches closer. "So that's why you didn't go to church, huh?" Molly instantly holds a likeness to Cruella de Vil and Mr. Hyde. Both proud and evil.

Dumbfounded, I grab hold of my backpack strap. "Who told you?"

"Greg. I met up with him in the hallway minutes ago, and he spilled the details. Your loss, my gain." She raises her jaw. "I've got a date with him tomorrow night as soon as practice is over."

I think, *Yesterday, I went out with Greg a.m. He had a date p.m. And now Molly.* I'm surprised how fast that boy gets around.

"Molly, before you get lost in your head. I've got a warning. My advice is be careful. A few minutes ago, I told him to take a good look at himself. I wouldn't go out with him again if he was the only guy on campus."

To protect myself from any further interrogation, I change the topic from me to her. "What about Josh? Aren't you two still together?"

Molly shifts her books from one arm to the next. "He understands."

I shake my head, hoping to gain understanding. "Since when? Did he say it was okay for you to go out with someone else? Who will you drool over next?"

She glares at me. "Don't be so quick to judge. The minute Jimmy went out of town, you jumped at the chance to go out with Greg. What do you have to say for yourself?"

Argh! Wish she would stop chasing me down like a prosecuting attorney. Molly taps her foot and waits for me to enter my plea.

"I'm guilty, but it wasn't like you said. You're not interested in facts. All you want is the juicy stuff. So I'll save my breath and explain everything to Jimmy when he gets home. We haven't been declared a "couple" like you and Josh. You once told me you couldn't imagine yourself with anyone else."

"Yeah—well, things have changed." She takes a deep breath and lets out a haughty sigh.

I nail her. "So now, suddenly, following lunch, you treat Josh like some discarded toy? I'm tired of you putting me on trial for details and then going on your merry way with a smirk on your face. I'm not going to let you derail me. I've got too many things on my slate that I'm trying to figure out."

Molly brushes a wrinkle from her H&M buckle jeans and runs for Building 5. After that emotional trial, I head for the building then dress into my track clothes.

As soon as I exit the girls' lockers, Coach Forsythe waves and calls me over. "Beth, I need to talk with you." I saunter over to the grandstands, where he sits and motions for me to join him. "What's going on? Are you okay?"

"Working through something, Coach. Why do you ask?"

"Because, Beth, you haven't been your sweet same self lately. You have been acting different. I'm glad that you qualified for the prelims in the 3,200-meter event, but what happened in your eight-hundred-meter race?"

I stare at the Verdugo Hills in the distance.

"After last week's practice, I thought you would nail both races on Saturday." Coach leans over his clipboard and waits for my answer.

I don't know why, but I tell about everything that's been going on with Molly and finish with, "Lately, Molly's acted like she's upset about something. Whenever the squad and I pump her with caring questions, she remains silent. She's been attacking me with verbal insults. I tried to shake my upset over Molly on Saturday. I thought that I had after finishing the 3,200, but then the thoughts about her anger toward me came rushing back during the eight hundred. I had a hard time focusing on the race."

"Maybe Molly's jealous."

"Could be, but I think there's something else brewing. The nasty remarks continue, and they hurt. What am I supposed to do?"

He sets the clipboard down. His face confident, nonjudgmental. "Sounds like you're doing all the right things. Keep going to church no matter what Molly or anyone else says. We are not supposed to understand what other people do. It's out of our control. God knows what she's doing. I'll be praying for you." He rests his elbows on his knees, draws his hands together to form a tepee, and places his closed mouth against the structure.

Surprised that Coach Forsythe knows about God, I feel comfortable to say, "Jimmy keeps telling me that he's praying for me. What does it mean?"

"Prayer is communication with God. When I go to God, I pray for people who don't know about Jesus and His love. Do you know Jesus, Beth?"

"Think I met him once." I watch Coach study the ground.

He lifts his head. "Beth, you should check Jesus out again. Let Him be the Lord and Savior of your life. He wants to help you and show you His plan. When you invite Jesus into your heart, you will experience peace. I pray you'll understand what you need to do so you can love—love yourself and others."

"How am I supposed to do that?"

"We can't love other people or ourselves the way we should unless we ask God for help. Remember that Molly or anyone else doesn't have the right to intimidate you into doing what they want so you'll be their so-called friend. It's hard, but learn to walk away and pray that Molly will let God touch her heart. You need to set up boundaries." He ends with a soft laugh. "Learning about perimeters is another lesson. You can have an appointment with me anytime."

"Thanks for listening."

"Thanks for opening up. One more thing: remember when I told you to run with perseverance?"

"Yeah."

"I meant it. Do your best at the prelims in May. Focus on what you've been taught and what you want to do." He stands. "Beth, you're smart and a good athlete. I believe you can qualify for the championship finals at the Cerritos College stadium. Keep trying, and don't worry.

"God says in Philippians 4:6 and 7, 'Do not be anxious about anything, but in every situation, by prayer and petition, with thanks-giving, present your requests to God. And the peace of God, which transcends all understanding, will guard your hearts and your minds in Christ Jesus.' It means that when you trust the Lord for every-thing, you will experience God's peace, which is far more wonderful than the human mind can understand."

Coach steps onto the track. "Today, I want you to go on a long run on the city sidewalks for an hour and a half with Josh to improve your aerobic fitness and endurance. Don't forget to cool down and stretch. I can train you to be a better athlete physically, but to be a better individual, you need to mature emotionally and spiritually."

I jog away, thinking about Coach Forsythe's words.

Chapter 15

The coach's words tumble around in my head all day Tuesday until the evening. Then I scribble notes about the events of the past few days into my diary and open the suitcase. My fingers come in contact with a small cold object. I open the clasp and stare at my reflection. What am I supposed to see in the mirror besides me? Wondering if Carol has a clue, I punch in her number.

"Hey, Carol. It's me, Beth."

"Hi, Beth."

I stare into the mirror and check my face for zits. "If you found a compact mirror, what would you look at?"

"Um, my makeup?"

"Give me another idea."

"Well, maybe you're supposed to look at what's behind your face—the good, the bad, the ugly?" A quiet moment slips by. "Beth, do you know when Jimmy's coming home?"

"Not sure. Are you on the prowl for Jimmy?"

"No, silly. I've been dating James. Jimmy told me how much he likes you."

I blow out a sigh of relief.

Carol continues, "I asked about Jimmy coming home because I wanted to know if you are still planning on coming to youth group even if Jimmy's still out of town tomorrow night. Cause if you are, I'd like to get to know you better."

"Yes, I'll be there. Let's squash the guys in volleyball."

After Carol says, "see you later," I rekey the title of my English paper, "Success… Looking at Your Heart," and think about the final paragraphs.

Tired from staying up late and working on my term paper, I zoom into the drive-through line at Starbucks Wednesday morning after taking Stephanie and RC to school. Angry about taking my siblings to school for the umpteenth time, I caution myself to calm down and think. *The kids are at Thomas Edison Elementary now; you've earned your space.* I pay for an extra shot of expresso in my mocha and an almond ginger biscotti, laced with a hint of lemon, and head for school.

Minutes later, I park in the student lot, put the coffee on the dashboard, turn off the ignition, then reach for my backpack on the floorboard. As I throw it over my shoulder, an edge of the canvas hits the drink. A waterfall of hot liquid forms and sends splashes from the light-brown brew and whipped cream to the steering wheel and floorboard. Large brown spots cover my jeans. I scream, "Ouch." Then I throw open the door and jump up and down. Brian comes from behind my car.

"What happened? Are you okay?"

"No." I point to the inside of my car.

Brian peeks over my shoulder to survey the damage. "Nasty."

"Now I've gotta go home and change. If I show up late for geometry, Max will mark me down as tardy and ask more questions."

Brian lays his hand on my shoulder and gives me a reassuring squeeze. "Sorry. I'll take you home so you can get paper towels to mop up."

"You sure?"

"Yeah." He pushes his glasses from the tip of his nose back onto the bridge. "If we hurry, we can be back before second period."

"Okay. I'll deal with Max tomorrow."

I lock my car and sprint to meet Brian already behind the wheel of his red Dodge pickup. The drive takes five minutes from the school lot to my house. Brian waits in the car while I hurry in to change.

In my room, I slip out of the drenched sky blue tee, navy cardigan, and jeans and rummage through my stash to find comfortable and dry, then fill my arms with the three items plus several items from my floor. Mom will be proud to see smaller piles. Next, I dash back down the stairs to the laundry room, where I throw my clothes in the washer, set it on gentle, eyeball about a fourth of a cup of detergent, and push the power button.

Satisfied with my accomplishment, I run into the kitchen, grab a roll of paper towels, and scoot back to Brian. When I slide onto the passenger seat, Brian snickers. Understanding the reason for his laugh, I punch him. "After I clean up my car, will you get me a second cup? If I get the same barista, I don't want to explain why I am there again."

He chuckles and winks. "Of course."

Minutes later, I mop up the mess in my car. Then rejoin Brian in his car and we head for the coffee kiosk. At the kiosk, Brian pays for the coffees and escorts me to a round table next to the building. The umbrella protects our skin from harmful UV rays. He takes a sip and wraps both hands around his cup. His shoulders relax. "Doctor is discharging Mom on Friday. It'll be nice to have her home." After another sip, he continues. "But it will be a few weeks before she's back to herself."

"Brian, I know it must've been scary when she had to go to the hospital and have those two surgeries. About two weeks ago, I woke from a bad dream about my dad. I woke up crying and yelling, 'Daddy, come back.' Although he never came home, I'm so glad your mom's on the mend and you're back at school." I reach for his hand. "Missed you, guy. "How have you and your dad been doing this week?"

Brian squeezes my hand and goes back to gripping his coffee. "Thanks for being there for me. You're sweet. This week has been, awful. Our schedule: stayed with Mom, came home, pulled out a microwave meal from the Stouffer's stack, heated it up, and ate dinner in front of the TV. Then we hurried back to the hospital for a couple of hours. When we got home, Dad headed for bed, and I tried to catch up on homework assignments. We're exhausted but happy the ordeal is over." Brian twists around on the bench and brings his legs to his chest. "What's it been like at your house?"

"Busy. It's always busy." I resist the urge to pour out my heart and tell him about how Mom and I got into it today. To relive the debate…worthless. I draw in a gulp of air and let it out. "Hey, did you hear any more about what or who caused the fire?"

"Yeah. Last night on the news the commentator said fire personnel believe someone was smoking in the closet where we keep the sheet music. The school, meaning the principal, has talked with a few suspects but no one has been charged with the crime."

Remembering that I kicked a carton of Marlboro cigarettes under Greg's passenger seat the other day, I choke as I swallow the last drop of coffee. I caution myself to not mention this to Brian because if Greg started the fire, I need more proof. Not knowing what to say as a follow up, I check the time on my cell. "We better head back to school."

Brian gathers the trash. We march arm in arm to the car.

Back on campus, I slip into PE just after the first bell and run to my locker to dress down. Molly approaches, gets in my face, and hollers like she's on the PA System. "Saw you go off campus with Brian."

Girls stop and gawk. They move on when I stare them down.

"So? What of it, Molly?" I'm tired of meeting this girl, now turned monster.

Molly crosses her arms and leans against the lockers to continue her questions with a syrupy voice. "Where did you guys go? What's the secret?"

"It's none of your business. You don't need to know 'cause no matter what I do, you find fault with it. I'm fed up with your attitude." I look straight at her. "Give me space."

Molly spins on her toe.

"Before you run off and have a field day about how mean I am, I have a question for you. Does Greg smoke?"

Molly bolts toward the gym. She barks, "Yeah, so what?" over her shoulder.

I'm glad that another clash with Molly is over, but what am I supposed to do with this info about Greg? My fear: another encounter with her at lunch.

With my lunch on a tray, I hurry to get under the canopy. Greg and Molly sit comfortably chatting at the squad's table. Molly turns my way with her lips spreading into a nasty "look at what I've got" line. She traces his collar with her index finger and turns to whisper in his ear.

With the taste of a sour lemon drop in my mouth, I take my tuna sandwich elsewhere. When Susan, Josh, and Brian rush up, I point to the squad's table. "Our table's been taken over by an alien."

The four of us dash to a picnic table at the far end of the cafeteria. Susan breathes a loud *pffff* and throws her backpack on the table and looks at Josh. "Josh, tell all. How come Molly's with Greg?"

Josh lifts his leg over the bench. "I'm history. Molly has a date with Greg today as soon as track practice is over. Maybe it's a good thing. Lately, I've been getting pretty tired of her whispers."

I share a convincing nod with the others. "Well, she'd better watch out. Her pompous peacock attitude might get her in trouble because she might be flirting with a criminal. Because Molly told me that Greg smokes."

Susan quickly turns her head around my way. "Are you thinking what I am thinking?"

"Like maybe he's responsible for the fire?"

"Yes."

All four of us turn our heads and watch the couple laugh and kiss. I say, "I hate the way she pokes her nose into things that are not her business. This morning in gym class, she blew up because I wouldn't tell her where I went with Brian."

Susan's eyebrows shoot toward the sky. Then she eyeballs Brian. "Where did you guys go? Tell only if you want to. No pressure." She smiles.

Out of the corner of my eye, I catch Brian grinning.

I catch her tease and jump in. "No pressure, huh? Well, Suze, because we're friends. I'll tell all. Our going off campus is funny now, but this morning it was embarrassing. Brian rescued me when my mocha fell off the dashboard and—"

"Got the picture: messy."

"Yeah. Brian took me home to change. We were back before second period. No big deal, but Molly was looking for some hot news. Stay away if you can help it."

"Thanks for the heads-up." Susan gives me a hug. "Don't want to get tangled in her web. She must be miffed about something very big."

"Right on. She's in a huff seven days a week. I wish she'd keep her anteater nose out of my business. My thoughts: she's clamming about past hurts. If she'd share all, she'd be happier and certainly easier to live with." Josh, Susan, and Brian raise their palms for a hand slap. "When she doesn't have her long her nose in the air, she can be fun."

Molly giggles loud enough to capture our attention. My group spins around to see the so-called happy couple sashay out of the lunch room.

"Tired of Molly's drama, I hope Pastor Rosenberg's sermon tonight will offer me some advice." I gulp water from my bottle. "Susan, will you come to youth group tonight?"

Susan stands to leave. "No. Got a history exam tomorrow—not my favorite subject. But I'll come on Sunday. You can count on it."

"What made you change your mind?"

"You."

"Me?"

"Yes, you. Because you've got problems and are looking for help. I think it might be a good place to get rid of my can of worms. I'd rather be like you and not like Molly—locked up inside. See you on the track. Later."

She waves.

"What about you, Brian? You up for youth group and church?"

"Not ready for the youth group, Beth. But will go to church on Sunday."

"Great."

Wednesday evening, the youth group sits around a table in the church's dining hall. I fill a vacant seat next to Carol.

"Beth, nice to have you back." Ty raises his palm; I slap it with a high five. "Missed you on Sunday."

My lips remain sealed.

Ty asks, "Beth, do you know when Jimmy is supposed to come home?"

Before I can say, "Dunno," Matthew cuts in. "Jimmy called last night and said he'll be back in school tomorrow."

One minute I'm ecstatic, and the next minute, fear sets in when I realize it might be time—time to reveal the whole truth, nothing but the truth. I need to prepare myself because after I share the Greg story, Jimmy might not want to be with me anymore. Maybe Carol will be his next choice because they've got something in common—God.

Carol offers me an oatmeal raisin cookie. My horrible thought sickens me. "No, thanks. Let's head for the gym."

"I'm glad you came back to youth group," Carol says as we stroll down the hall toward the gym. "Everyone likes you. I think we'll have a great time together this summer."

"Summer?"

"Yeah, the group has volunteered to help out at Special Olympics. When the youth group learned two years ago that I have a brother who has intellectual and physical disabilities, they thought it would be cool to volunteer. My brother Bryce is twenty but he has the mental capacity of a six-year-old and suffers from a rare heart condition. But you should see him in the pool. He slices the water faster than a dolphin. Trophies and ribbons, too many to count, decorate his bedroom walls.

"When we finish helping out for three days, the group has made plans to spend a week at Hume Lake, which is east of Fresno. The activities will include disc golf, boating, paint balling, a high ropes course, water games, and hiking. Other things will fill the three month break from school but don't know details yet—still in the works."

"Sounds like fun. I feel accepted here." Hope Mom will give up her babysitter so I can have some real fun. "What's the sermon about tonight?"

"Don't know, but think it has something to do with looking at ourselves from the inside out."

Suddenly, I feel a chill. Carol opens the door to the gym and announces to her team, "The guys are already on the court. Let's not let them win again," I give her a high five, dismiss my thoughts until church, and then take my place on the court.

The girls win with a score of twenty five to fifteen. Then Matthew kicks the ball toward a corner. "We lost because we were down one player."

Carol mocks, "Yeah, right."

The group laughs.

Eager to hear Pastor Rosenburg's message, I lead the group into the sanctuary. When the last song ends, Pastor Rosenburg walks his tall frame to the pulpit. "The title of my sermon is 'Face in the Mirror.' What would be your response to the following questions if Jesus asked you, 'How did you treat your wife, husband, child, mother, father, sister, or brother this morning? Do you put yourself before others? Does your attitude reflect an angry or calm disposition?'" The pastor pauses to sip water from his glass.

The back of my chair—stiff. The fabric on the seat causes poison oak itches.

The pastor continues, "Jesus knows how we will respond to problems, questions, and or people. He wants us to come to Him for every need. Each word in the Bible is attached to Jesus's love for you and me. Because we are human, we will always have sins like anger, jealousy, and loneliness tapping at the door of our hearts. If we choose to entertain them, we become depressed and wonder how we will survive the downer attitudes that we've adopted.

"When you accept Jesus as Lord and Savior, the Holy Spirit helps you with daily struggles, whatever they may be—like the loss of a loved one, relationship problems, tests in school, hard choices, or whatever."

Who told him about me? He nailed my problems.

The pastor swallows. "If you accepted Jesus as your Lord and Savior a long time ago, you can rededicate your life to Him today. If don't feel a closeness, it's probably because you walked away. If you feel God's gentle touch tonight…"

Overcome with emotion, I fail to hear what he was going to say next. My vision blurs with pools of tears. I hyperventilate, bend over, force in air, and exhale slowly. Carol leans over. "Are you okay?"

I shake my head and fish for Kleenex in my purse, jerk out three, and blow my nose. The sound of a small horn reverberates through the sanctuary. "I need to leave."

In the foyer, I sit on the couch, lean my forehead against folded arms, and let the dam break. Between tears, I manage to say, "There's so much I don't understand. I wish there was a quick fix." Hiccups follow. "I…I feel so slow…'cause I can't figure things out. I'm… tired. Need to go home…think about this Jesus stuff."

"Okay." Carol reaches into her hot-pink leather bag and draws out a thin square box wrapped in white tissue paper and tied with a red ribbon. "Got this for you this afternoon. Wait till you get home to unwrap it. Please call me tomorrow. Because—"

The hiccups quit. "I know. You'll be praying for me. Don't stop." I wrap my fist around the Kleenex and dash for the car. And home.

When I open the front door at nine thirty, the house is still. Glad Mom's not around. Don't feel like talking. I tiptoe up the stairs. The latch catches with a faint click. I tear off the wrapping from Carol's gift and place the CD into the player and listen. The artist asks, "Are you tired of trying to solve problems on your own? Why not trust God, for everything?"

My answer to the artist's question: I'm not sure I can trust God. I thought the contents from the suitcase were going to erase my pain, but they have just confused me.

With a tear slithering down my cheek, I cautiously remove the ninth item from the mouth of the suitcase. An antique handkerchief has the words "I Love You" on one corner. The opposite corner reads, "For those tears I died." The words are printed in red—blood red.

Chapter 16

In the morning, after tossing and turning and spending a few fitful hours of sleep over what to do with the antique hand-kerchief, I still don't understand what I'm supposed to do. Confused and exhausted, I slowly come down the stairs. Mom rests against the kitchen counter and files a pink chipped fingernail. She looks up from her hands. Her face is stern. "Sit down, young lady."

"Mom, what happened?"

She points to a chair. Nervous over about what is to follow, I hurry to the fridge, pour myself a glass of OJ, carry it to the table, and plop my body onto my chair.

Mom looks daggers at me. "I found your blue clothes along with my sweater, which used to be white, in the washer. Didn't you look in the machine before you threw your clothes in?" She slides onto the seat across from me.

I choke on OJ and slap my chest. My breath comes out in a whoosh. "Whoops. Sorry, I didn't see it. I'll be more careful next time I throw something in the washer."

"The sweater was a gift from Robert." Mom folds her arms and glares. "It had been through the cycle. I was going to put it on a hanger to let it air-dry when I came home for lunch." Pause. "Explain yourself."

"Sorry. I spilled mocha all over myself, so I rushed home to change."

"Need I remind you that you're not the only one living in this house?"

I shake my head sheepishly.

Mom continues, "Reimbursement will come out of your allowance."

"Okay. Okay."

"Your attitude has to stop. You need to be more respectful of the other people in this house. And about your notes—after the first note we found on the floor, I asked you to tell us where you were headed, who you would be with, and what time we could expect you home. You have continued to fail to do what we asked. Are you so into yourself that you haven't listened?"

"When I wrote the notes, I was rushed. *Sorry.*" I shove the glass of juice away; juice sloshes over the rim of the glass. Mom scowls. I get up, rush to the counter, grab paper towels, and hurry back to the table to mop up the orange lake.

"And another thing," Mom says looking at me. "I want you to talk to me."

I quit mopping and throw the orange towels down. Fuming, I say loudly. "Me? Talk to you? Hah. I keep trying to get you alone and tell me about Daddy. But every time I ask for time, RC or Steph shows up. And you come up with, 'Not now, Beth, but I'll think of something that we can do together.' You have said that in different ways three times."

A minute flies by. "What's wrong, Beth?"

Tears skip down my cheeks. "Mom, I tried to remind you weeks ago that you and I use to spend time together. And that I missed Daddy's hugs and wanted to know what happened to him? You never explained. Bma gave me 'time.' Now this thing with Brian's Mom and Jimmy's grandma. Why can't you and Robert give me time to listen to my heart. I'm tired of being the live-in babysitter. I fear I won't see my friends or have a life when the baby comes."

Mom laughs and motions for me to come and sit on her lap. I give in. She brushes my hair with her fingers. "I apologize for being preoccupied with my job, Beth. I will arrange my schedule so I'm not asking you to help out so often. As far as Robert goes, he and I have been talking. He's working on being a better communicator. He really thinks you're a great kid, outside of your notes." She winks and gives me a squeeze. "I think you'll see a new Robert when he returns from this trip."

She swallows. "It's time for us to have a real date. Would you like to go to dinner tomorrow night? I will see if Steph and RC can spend a few hours with Mrs. Cummings."

I double blink. "Just you and me? Where we can talk about Dad at dinner?"

"Yes and yes. Sorry I didn't ask the neighbor a week ago to sit Steph and RC so you and I could shop for a dress. Will you forgive my brain freeze?"

"Yes. You're forgiven, Mom."

"Beth, I need something from you."

"Anything. What do you want?"

"Will you change your hostile attitude toward Robert?"

"I'll try." I kiss her cheek. Then glancing at the orange Brawny towels still on the table, I say, "Jimmy and I had an issue the other night at the dance. He's coming home today, and I need to clear up something that was misunderstood. Would it be okay if I meet with him around six for a couple of hours? And after church last night, I have a few God questions."

"God questions?"

"Mom, I'll bring you up to date when I come home tonight."

"Look forward to it. Sure, go ahead."

I jump up from Mom's lap when RC and Stephanie bolt into the kitchen. My youngest sibling asks, "What's for breakfast?"

Mom looks into my bro's brown eyes. "Eggo waffles. They'll be ready soon." Then she rises from her chair and looks my way. "See what you mean, Beth. It is a busy house."

❋ ❋ ❋

I drive into the student lot, honk, and wave to Jimmy as he emerges from his car. He looks my way. I snatch my stuff and rush to greet him with a nervous but powerful hug. His arms hang like wet spaghetti. "Glad you're home."

Jimmy remains tight-lipped.

I swallow a lump. "Sorry about your grandma."

"Appreciate your sympathy," Jimmy says after locking the car. Then he walks quickly toward Building 4 for his first class.

I sprint to catch up. "Got a few questions. Could we hang out after track practice?"

"Guess."

"How does Kentucky Fried sound for a picnic in the park?"

"Whatever." He picks up his steps. His red shirt disappears around the corner.

I bite the inside of my cheek and head for geometry, choosing to understand that *whatever* means sure.

Mr. Max sits at his desk, unaware of my presence until I pass him the note that Mom wrote explaining my absence yesterday. He looks up and clears his throat. "Thank you. Take a seat."

When the last student is seated, Mr. Max gets up and brings the class to order. "Put your books away. Get ready for a pop quiz." Moans and groans from my fellow classmates agree with my gut reaction.

I quickly scribble the answer to the last question. If my time with Jimmy goes as smoothly as the test, I'll be worry free. The remaining minutes of geometry whiz by.

Thankfully, physical education and Spanish post no warning signs of a Molly approaching. Finally, the long-awaited lunch bell does its thing. With the energy of Wile E. Coyote, I run to the outside eating area.

As I round the corner, continuous wails pierce my ears. Anxious to investigate, I quicken my steps toward the squad, toss my backpack on the ground, and slide in next to Jimmy. Molly buries her head in her hands and wails louder. "Why are you crying?"

Molly looks up, snapping. "What do you care?"

"Come on, Molly. What happened?"

Susan explains, "Greg was hit by a drunk driver last night."

At the mention of his name, I freeze and avoid Jimmy's eyes. My gut tells me that this is not the time to share what I know about Greg. I ask, trying to be sympathetic, "Is he hurt?"

"Well, you might as well know." Molly sniffles and rummages around in her backpack. She brings up a handful of Kleenex. "I don't know how Todd"—she stops midsentence and sneaks a look at Susan.

Susan's eyebrows knit and form a "V" on the lower part of her forehead. Her eyes turn into narrow slits, her lips press together and wrinkles appear.

Molly wipes a tear and picks up where she left off. "Found out, but Greg has a bunch of broken bones and may be paralyzed from the waist down. His Mercedes is totaled. He's at the Glendale Memorial Hospital and Health Center."

"Horrible." I fish for more words, but none come. Susan bites her lip. Brian traces imaginary objects with his finger on the table. Josh's eyes cast a blank stare. From Jimmy's look, I can almost visualize the questions that stand in the trenches between his brows.

Josh asks simply, "Molly, are you going to the hospital?"

"Duh." She gathers her books and dashes out of the cafeteria.

I look around, and everyone looks back at me, speechless. Jimmy rises, lifts each long leg over the bench, and chases down a buddy. Josh, Susan, Brian, and I hurry off to classes.

❄ ❄ ❄

At the end of the day, I spot Jimmy heading toward his car. Anxious thoughts cause me to run after him. Encased in a web of fear, I ask, "Jimmy, are we still going to the park?"

He continues to walk. Then with his back to me, Jimmy unlocks the driver's door. "If that's what you want."

I stand off to the side, picking at a broken nail. "Will you follow me home?"

Jimmy throws his books in the back seat, gets in, closes the door, and unrolls the window. "Okay." Then he starts the engine.

My brain—confused. Should I be excited about dinner in the park, or worry about Jimmy's quiet distance? I fumble for my keys and sprint to my car. When I pull onto my driveway, Jimmy remains in his car with the engine idling. I slide in on his passenger seat.

After ordering from KFC in the drive-through lane, Jimmy drives slowly to the park. Only the aroma of greasy roasted chicken hangs in the air.

A slight breeze meets us at the front entrance of the park as Jimmy and I walk under the white arch supported by huge pillars. In the distance, children act like monkeys on the jungle gym and mothers push toddlers on the swing sets. In front of me, a child cries after a fall, stands, and watches blood drip down his leg. His mother kneels, wipes his wound, and tries to console him. "Don't worry, Tommy. It'll be okay."

After looking at Tommy's blood, I remember the words on the handkerchief from the suitcase. "For those tears, I died."

Jimmy nudges me. "Let's grab a table."

Ready to spill all the details of my sorry life, I spread a paper Valentine's Day tablecloth over the worn wooden slats of the nearest table and hope Jimmy will listen and forgive. He makes no comment about the red heart in the middle of the tablecloth when he sets the meal on the table. Then without glancing at me, he pops the caps of the two ginger ale bottles and takes a long slug from his drink and sits on the bench. I drop down next to him.

Jimmy moves away, making the space between us larger, but he turns and faces me. He runs his hand around his jaw. "Beth, when you suggested we meet, I wasn't keen about the idea. But now, I'm glad we're here. Before you tell me what's on your mind, I need to and want to pray."

My heart pounds against my chest louder than drums during half time at a football game. My gut tells me he found out about Greg. Someone must've blabbed. I pick at a broken nail, close my eyes, and bow my head.

Jimmy prays, "Thank You, Father, for the breeze to cool us from the heat of the day. Help Beth and I to be honest about the things You want us is to share. Thank You for the food. Amen." He opens his eyes. Suspecting he noticed my wet eyes, he asks, "What's the matter?"

I swallow. "I need to… I mean… I don't know where to begin. You'll hate me forever."

"Won't hate you. Start from the beginning."

I push the plate of food away. Sweat forms on my brow but force myself to look into his blue eyes. "Jimmy, I apologize for leaving you standing at the dance and going with Susan. She wanted to show me the new guy on campus—Greg, the one who was in the accident. I never wanted to hurt you or ruin the evening. After your call on Sunday, he called and wanted me to show him the ocean."

"I know all about it."

I close my mouth before a fly looks for shelter from the heat. "Molly?"

"Yes. On the way home from the airport last night, I ran into the store to get milk for Mom. I met Molly in the checkout line."

"She's so quick to inflict suffering. She doesn't know that I ended up calling Mom for a ride home." After a long exhale, I add, "Did she mention that on Monday I told Greg to disappear from my life forever?"

"No."

"Of course not. She's only into what she wants to hear. Is that the reason I got no phone call when you got home, no hug this morning, and the cold shoulder at lunch."

"Yep, and that along with being treated like I had chicken pox at the dance. Never thought you'd think about another guy. I was more than hurt. Didn't know how to explain the depth of my anger, jealousy, and bitterness, so I held it in until now. I've been clutching pride like a child with a brand new toy.

"Beth, if it wasn't for you asking to have dinner tonight, I might still be self-pitying. You wanted to talk in the car after the dance, but I wouldn't let you and said, 'Not now.' Can you forgive me for not being upfront with you?"

The tenderness in his heart—unlike anyone else. "Absolutely. Then because we are being candid with one another, I share all feelings. "Since the day I met you, Jimmy, it's been my wish that we'd be a couple someday. I'm so, so very sorry for what I did." My hands shake. I hold my breath, waiting for Jimmy's response.

"Beth, I'm sorry for not getting excited to meet. You say you want to be a couple, but what happens if another guy comes along?"

"Trust me. It'll never, never happen. I've learned a lot about reptiles. What happens if another girl walks by?"

"Not to worry, Beth. I know I've got gold right here. Don't want anyone else." Jimmy inches over and pulls me in. I don't resist. Our lips meet. Even though the kiss isn't under the stars, it's genuine. And *so* worth waiting for.

After a long minute, Jimmy pulls back. "I forgive you. Beth, will you be my girl?"

"Yes. Yes. I forgive you too, Jimmy. But I need to admit a few more things."

"Okay."

"The day you left, my life—Titanic. Sorry I didn't know what to say to you when you told me about your grandma. All I could think of was my own pain. Sorry for my selfishness." Heat rushes to my cheeks. "For the last three days, I've wondered about my life. Not getting answers about my dad and new problems caused me to think I was headed for the junkyard. Then when I found a mirror in the suitcase and listened to Pastor Rosenburg's sermon last night, 'Face in the Mirror,' I was shocked at the timing. I thought more about God."

"Sounds like you've had a pretty rough week."

"Beyond difficult. I need to tell you more."

Jimmy waits quietly.

"In Miss Marvel's class, even though I didn't understand everything the teacher said, I invited Jesus into my heart because I wanted someone to love me, but I really didn't understand the full meaning of what it means to believe and follow Christ. Then after talking with Coach Forsythe—who encouraged me to invite Jesus into my heart and make him a permanent resident—Pastor Rosenburg's sermons, a mirror, and a handkerchief with the words, "For those tears I died" from the suitcase last night, I'm ready now to invite Jesus into my heart for real." I pick peeling paint from the table to gather my thoughts.

"Jimmy, will you pray with me?"

"Of course." He reaches for and holds both of my hands.

I pray. "Jesus, I'm sorry I walked away from You. I confess that I've been angry toward You and Mom. I've lied to Coach Forsythe,

Sergeant Hoffman, Mom, and Carol. Please forgive all my sins. Thank You for whoever left the suitcase. I'm grateful because it brought me back to You. Thank You for submitting to the Father's will and allowing the Romans to nail You to the cross, and for shedding every ounce of your blood and dying for me. Thank You for rising from the grave. I look forward to living with You in Heaven as a child of God.

"Help me to live my life the way You want. Jesus come into my heart and be my Lord and Savior. Thank You for forgiving me of all sins. I pause to blow my nose. "I need a favor: Please let Mom explain at dinner tomorrow night about Daddy and why he never came home. Amen." Then I add, "Please forgive me, Lord, for taking so long to understand what You wanted me to do. I'm sorry I was so stupid. I won't turn away even if things, life, get *scary*."

I look up and see Jimmy's eyes misting over. He smiles. "Praise God." Then he bows his head. "Thank You, God, for convicting me of my sins. I am sorry for my dishonesty, anger, bitterness, and jealousy. In obedience to 1 John 1:9, which says, 'If we confess our sins, he is faithful and just and will forgive us our sins and purify us from all unrighteousness,' I receive Your forgiveness, Lord, for my pride. Thank You for Beth and her understanding. Thank You that she is now a child and an heir of God. I love You, Amen." After a moment, Jimmy says, "Beth, explain *scary*."

"You know like when we don't know what to do."

He looks deep into my eyes. "Beth, you shouldn't feel foolish about not coming to Christ sooner than you did. Everything is in God's hands including the timing. When you came, minutes ago, it was perfect—your words were real." Jimmy pauses. "Fear will always try to take the joy of knowing and walking with Jesus away, but don't let it trip you up. Wherever you are, God will take care of you. One of my favorite verses is, 'I call to God and the Lord saves me. Evening, morning, and noon I cry out in distress and he hears my voice.' It's found in Psalm 55:16 and 17."

"Thank you." A quiet relaxes me. I fold up the tablecloth and bring it to my chest.

Jimmy reaches for my hand and pulls me in for another soft, sweet kiss. "Let's celebrate your newness by going out for ice cream."

"You're on. Please, any ice cream flavor but Rocky Road. Been there."

Chapter 17

"Jimmy, thanks for the ice cream and the talk."

He backs out of the driveway. A soft breeze carries, "You're welcome. Anytime."

I watch his car turn the corner, I press my hand on the back of the front door and guide it slowly to the lock. Hearing soft snores coming from the living room, I tiptoe in to see Mom sleeping soundly in the La-Z-Boy overstuffed couch. Guess I'll have to wait to share the good news. I remember that she needs her sleep for the baby she's carrying, I back out of the room and rest my foot on the first step of the stairs.

A sleepy, raspy voice questions, "Beth?"

I run to her. "Sorry. Was trying to be quiet."

Mom sits up and pats the couch cushion. "Come join me. Nap time is over."

I wiggle into a spot on the other end of the couch, pull the soft white crocheted afghan over my legs, and face her. "Dinner with Jimmy was the best ever." I weave an end of yarn back into the blanket. "Know we plan to talk tomorrow night, but I need to tell you what I did tonight."

Mom's eyes widen.

"Don't get worried. It's good. Remember when Grandma Bma took me to church?"

Mom nods.

"Well, after a few Sundays, the Sunday school teacher told me about Jesus and how much He loved me. Needing love, I asked Him to come into my heart and prayed He would take away the pain of Daddy's disappearance. Instead, He took Grandma Bma. My pain grew. I got angrier."

Mom gasps and blows it out. "Beth, I'm so sorry."

131

I wave at a nonexistent fly in the air and brush a tear from my lower lid. "Mom, it's okay. I didn't like my stinkin' attitude, but I had to figure out how to surrender my pain and anger to God. When I found the suitcase, I thought the traveling box held answers to my aches. But after drawing out seven items from the mouth of the suitcase, I felt alone, like I was stranded on a steep incline at Mount Shasta because I didn't understand anything. My questions multiplied and looked like the rocks and rugged terrain. I got more frustrated than a child who can't find his way home.

"Then on Monday, the suitcase gave up a mirror. The item coupled with Pastor Rosenburg's sermons encouraged me to really look at myself." I yawn. "I'm still having trouble understanding the whys of the first six items."

Mom scratches her brow. "The suitcase may not have been there only for you."

"What do you mean?"

"Well, as you tell others about the suitcase and Jesus, they may find themselves wondering what needs to be changed in their lives."

I throw off the afghan and straighten. "Mom, you just solved a question I had. When I found the suitcase, there was a letter attached. In the letter, whoever wrote it said, 'It only takes a spark to get a fire going.' I didn't understand the meaning until now. I think it means that if I share Jesus and His love, it becomes contagious and others will want to know Him. Thank you, Mom."

"I didn't know I was a problem solver, but you're welcome." Mom rests her head against the back cushion. "Maybe?"

"Maybe what?"

"Maybe the kids and I will join you at church. I'll let you know."

I clap my hands. "Great." I move over to give her a hug and then retreat to my corner of the couch. "Last week Jimmy told me about a picture in the Christian bookstore. He said the picture shows Jesus standing and knocking at a closed door. The knob is on the inside. The door represents a human heart."

Mom cries softly.

"What's the matter?"

She grabs a tissue off the side table. "I've seen the picture before but never knew what it meant. Please go on with your story." She sniffles.

"On Wednesday, I unfolded an antique handkerchief when I pulled it out of the suitcase. The words 'I love you' and 'For those tears I died' were written in blood red on two corners. This afternoon I prayed with Jimmy, surrendered my heart and life to Jesus, and promised I will not turn away.

"I've still got questions, but now, the anger and pain—not so much."

Waves of tears rush down Mom's and my cheeks. My voice cracks. "Please pass me a tissue. What a picture we must make."

Mom laughs as she passes me the box of tissues. "Yeah, but it feels good to let it all out and get my daughter back. I've missed you."

"You mean our talks?"

She nods.

I move over next to Mom and put my head on her shoulder. "Missed you too. I'm so sorry, Mom, for the way I've acted." It feels good to really say and mean it.

"Honey, I forgive you. When you're done with the suitcase, will you tell me what else you learned?"

"Definitely. My days with the suitcase—intimidating, challenging, exciting."

"Beth, I love you very much. I believe in you. You're smart and have lots of potential."

"Coach, Jimmy, and even Mr. Max said the same thing. It feels good to know that I have people in my corner who are rooting for me."

"Can I be your biggest fan?"

"Sorry, Mom, you come in second. I've given Jesus first place."

The grandfather chimes eleven thirty. Mom nudges me. "We'd better get to bed. You've got school in the morning."

"Thanks for listening. Love you."

She stands and drapes the afghan over the back of the couch. "I love you too. Hope I can answer your questions tomorrow night."

"No worries, Mom." I kiss Mom on the cheek before I climb the stairs.

Tired but not sleepy and pumped beyond words about dinner with Mom tomorrow night, I open the suitcase. The yellow glow from my lamp reveals the identity of not one but two things. The first, a cross made out of two rough splintered sticks. The second, a soft red leather Bible. Then I understand another reason for the suitcase. The one who left the suitcase was trying to show me that I should depend on Jesus for everything. Tears well up in my eyes. "Thank You, Lord Jesus. What do You want to tell me tonight?"

I lay the cross on the carpet and slide a red ribbon from the third chapter in the Gospel of John. The words in the sixteenth verse are underlined. "For God so loved the world that he gave his one and only Son, that whoever believes in him shall not perish but have eternal life." At the end of the verse, "See Psalm 139 verses one through four" is written in blue ink.

Because I'm a new believer and don't know the Bible, I turn to the table of contents for help. I read down until I find the word "Psalm." Then I fan the pages until I come to the chapter. It says:

> You have searched me, Lord, and know me. You
> know when I sit and when I rise, you perceive
> my thoughts from afar. You discern my going out
> and my lying down; you are familiar with all my
> ways. Before a word is on my tongue you, Lord,
> know it completely.

I bow my head. Through tears I pray aloud, "Thank You, Jesus, for loving me, knowing everything about me, for caring so much. Thank You for loving me, for teaching, and guiding me to Your truth. I know You will be in the restaurant before I get there tomorrow. I really believe You will help me get closure. Thank You for Mom and our talk tonight."

Then seeing that it's after midnight, I change clothes, set the alarm, turn off the light, and crawl between the sheets.

✳ ✳ ✳

Ring! Ring! Ring! wakes me. I yell, "Okay, okay, I'm up." I grab the alarm and shut it off with a slap, then rub sleep from my eyes. Smells of sizzling pork float into my room from the space between the beige carpet and the door and forces me to dress in a hurry.

When I throw open my door, Mom's voice echoes from downstairs. "Kids, come and get it while it's hot."

I zip down the stairs into the kitchen. "What's for breakfast? Smells fabulous. I'm famished."

Mom drops a teabag into a cup and turns her head. "No meetings this morning. Following our talk last night, work now follows my family's needs. A Dutch baby is in the oven. The recipe said to whisk eggs, flour, and milk in the blender and bake it." She turns on the oven light; we both crouch down and look through the glass. Mom holds up the cookbook. "Beth, it looks like the picture in the cookbook, a fluffy pancake. You think?"

"Yes, Mom."

Jubilant with her success, Mom stands and points to the table. "There's powdered sugar, raspberry jam, and salsa for the topping." She spins back around and forks sausage links from the skillet, drops them on a plate, and hands it to me. "Please put this on the table and pour juice for all of us."

While pouring the juice, I think about how nice it is to have a likeness of Julia Child back in the kitchen. "Mom, are we still on for tonight?"

Stephanie and RC come around the corner in stocking feet and take their places at the table. Mom says, "Looking forward to it."

"Forward to what?" Stephanie asks.

Mom lifts the Dutch baby from the oven and cuts it into four servings. "Mrs. Cummings is going to watch you and RC for a few hours while Beth and I go to dinner."

RC sets his glass of juice back on the table after taking a drink. "Why can't we go too?"

"Because I need to spend time with Beth. My plan is to spend more time with each of my kids. When you finish eating and get dressed, I'll take you and your sister to school on my way to work."

The kids yell in unison, "Yippee!"

They're not the only ones excited. I'm deliriously happy. Mom brings the meal to the table, places it on the yellow tablecloth, and sits next to me. A voice in my head asks, *Are you going to thank the Lord for the food?*

I swallow a bite. "May I pray before we eat?"

Stephanie and RC freeze with forks in their mouths. Mom lays down her fork. "Sure."

Looking like chipmunks with stored food in their cheeks, the kids lay down the utensils.

"Thank You, Jesus, for this day and this wonderful breakfast. Thank You for changes. Amen." A quiet minute. "Can't wait to see what you are going to cook next, Mom."

"You'll have to wait and see. It felt good to get the cookbooks out again, Beth."

"Thanks for breakfast," I say after swallowing the last bite. Then I dash up the stairs and throw my backpack over one arm. A corner of the suitcase catches my eye. I can't resist. The next item is a running shoe. Coach Forsythe's words echo in my head: "Run with perseverance." On the way out of my room, I whisper, "Thank You, Jesus, for the coach and this shoe that encourages me to keep walking, running to follow You. Amen."

❋ ❋ ❋

After an easy morning in my classes, I rush up to Jimmy in the hall and put my hands over his eyes, "Guess who?"

He spins around with his award winning smile. "I know your touch, Beth. How are you today?"

"Couldn't be better."

"On your way to lunch?"

"Sure am."

I glance up into his gentle blues. "Again, thanks for the park."

"No prob. Glad you felt comfortable enough to share with me. You've done a lot of work to search for your answers. Excited you came back to Jesus."

"You're not the only one who's more than exited." I squeeze his hand.

Jimmy winks and rubs his forehead."

"What's going on in that brain of yours?"

"Are you busy tomorrow?"

"No plans."

"Beth, would you spend the day with me? We haven't just hung out for a long time."

"What did you have in mind?" I cock my head and look at him from the corner of my eyes. "Does hanging out have anything to do with working on the car?"

"No. The sanding and priming are done. The car's engine is at the machine shop. When it comes back, Dad is going to teach me how to install and tune it up. You can help this summer, if you want."

"I want. But what about tomorrow?"

When we approach the lunchroom, the noise intensifies. Jimmy raises his voice, "Would you like to take a drive to Santa Monica for the day? I'll make dinner reservations at the Ocean Avenue Seafood Restaurant. It overlooks the ocean. Are you up for it?"

"Absolutely. Sounds fun. I'll call you when I get home today as soon as I check in with Mom."

Jimmy drops my hand and cups my elbow in his palm. "Let's get in line."

While waiting for our turn at the salad bar, I fill Jimmy in on the latest. "In addition to Josh, Susan is planning on coming to church this Sunday."

He takes two steps backward. "Did I hear you right? After Brian said he would come, now it's Josh and Susan? For real?"

"For real." Aware several eyes are looking my way, I lower my voice. "And Mom is thinking about bringing the kids too."

"Wow." He gives me a hug and a soft kiss on the cheek.

The kid behind Jimmy pleads. "Move on."

Jimmy and I exchange smiles. He pays the cashier for our meals, then I follow him to the table. Molly stares at me with her piercing dark brown eyes. "Why are you hugging and kissing in line?"

Jimmy glances at me from the corner of his laughing eyes. "Molly, we're taking care of unfinished business."

Jimmy and I laugh aloud. I think, *finally, Molly appears to have lost her tongue.* I ask, "How's Greg?"

Tears pour. Inaudible words float to the surface from below Molly's tidal wave of tears. I reach for her hand. She pulls away. "Went to the hospital last night. Greg's doctor confirmed that he's paralyzed from the waist down. He'll be in physical therapy forever." Molly wails. "And he might be in trouble. One of the teachers reported that she saw Greg loitering on the school grounds between periods on the day of the fire. He told her he was looking for the office so he could register for classes."

"Is his dad or mom at the hospital?"

"His dad is out of town. Don't know if his mom is on her way or has even been told. Doesn't someone from the hospital call family members?"

Jimmy jumps in. "Yes, a minister or someone on the pastoral staff immediately informs the family."

Josh swallows a bite of apple. "Molly, do you want to come to church on Sunday?"

She spits venomous words. "Oh, no. Now they've got you going too." She plops her milk carton down on the table hard. White liquid drips through the slats onto the concrete below. "You can have it. I'm not interested." She gathers her trash, throws her backpack over her shoulder, and runs toward a dark hallway.

Voices and the clatter of dishes come to an immediate standstill when Molly trips and falls over an extended leg stretched out from one of the benches. She pushes all hands of help away.

At the end of the day, Jimmy walks me to my car after a hard workout on the track. I press my back against the driver's side of his car and look up into his eyes. "Would you pray for me tonight? It might be rough. Mom and I still have some unsolved issues to talk about."

"You've always got my prayers, Beth."

"Thanks. What time will you pick me up in the morning?"

"How's ten sound?"

"Great. Can't wait. I'll pack a lunch. Weather forecast: low eighties."

We part, and I rush to jump in behind the wheel and head for home. I'm so pumped. Life is great. Got Jesus, a boyfriend, and a date with Mom.

❋ ❋ ❋

At home, Mom stands over the sink and splashes water over carrots, celery, tomatoes, and cucumbers in the colander. My mood turns to panic. "Are we going to dinner?"

"Yes."

My body relaxes.

"I'm putting together a salad to go with the pizza I ordered for the kids to take over to the neighbor's house for supper. The kids want their favorite, as always."

We chime together, "Cheese," and laugh.

I slide onto my chair. "Jimmy wants to take me to Santa Monica tomorrow. Would it be okay?"

Mom dries her hands and sits next to me. "Yes, you can go. Don't have anything, except Steph's dance lessons"—her blue eyes sparkle—"which I will take her to." She pauses. "What time are you leaving?"

"Tenish. I'll be gone all day. Jimmy wants to celebrate my coming back to Jesus at a cool restaurant for dinner."

"Hope you have a great time," Mom says. Then she looks like she's gathering her thoughts. "I'd like to join you for church on Sunday. Do they have Sunday school for the kids?"

I throw my arms around Mom's neck. "Wonderful. Fantastic. Fabulous. Yes, there is Sunday school for all ages." My heart skips a beat. "What time are the reservations tonight?"

"I made reservations for two at the Smoke House for seven."

Chapter 18

om holds the restaurant's dark oak door open. I slip inside, my heels sink into the thick padding of the rustic brown-and-black plaid wall to wall lobby carpet. Piano music floats to my ears. The tune is unrecognizable, but calming. Pictures of movie stars, young and old, dot the walls. Makes sense because it's across from Warner Bros. movie studio. "Nice, huh?"

"Yeah, and nostalgic." It's a perfect, quiet setting for what I need to talk about.

Stepping up to the desk, Mom announces our arrival. "I'm Mrs. Cade. I have reservations for two at seven."

The maître d' slides her index finger down a page until she finds the name. "Yes, Mrs. Cade, your table's ready. Please follow me." She leads us to a quiet table in the back and away from the bar.

Mom and I slide onto the cranberry-ice leather-tufted booth. The hostess places menus in each of our hands. "Enjoy your meals. Your waiter will be with you in a moment." She saunters off.

I fold the menu, lay it on top of my plate, and slide my palm over the crisp white linen tablecloth. "Mom, this place is so perfect, beautiful. Glad we came."

"I wanted an intimate place so we could talk over dinner."

The waiter arrives. "My name's Erik. Have you decided, or do you need more time?"

Mom says, "More time, please."

"Take all the time you need. May I get drinks?"

Mom orders herbal tea; I ask for a diet Coke. Erik leaves smiling. After a quiet moment, I say, "Mom, do you do remember where we went after my ballet class each week?"

"Of course. We ate a picnic lunch then walked around Echo Park. You fed the mallard ducks the fresh bread from the bakery. One of the bakers, Doc James, at Vons grocery store had a loaf ready on

141

Wednesdays and Fridays. When he saw you skipping down the aisle, he greeted you with, 'Good morning, blond bomber. Are you ready for the park?' Do you remember?"

Erik delivers the drinks.

"Mom, I remember. But I had forgotten the nickname he gave me until now." My eyes follow the bubbles in my Coke as they race to the surface and burst. "Mom—"

Mom inhales and exhales. "We'll talk and share more in a minute? But right now, we'd better think about what we want to eat. I suspect Erik will return soon."

Don't like the stall, but then I see Erik heading for our table.

"Ladies, are you ready or do you need more time?"

"No, I mean yes, I'm ready." He grins at my slip. "I'd like prime rib, medium rare, and a baked potato with all of the fixings, please."

He nods and focuses on Mom.

"I'd like the special for the night: grilled salmon with lime butter." Mom lifts her eyes from the menu. "What do you think, Beth? Should we get Caesar salads and a full order of their famous garlic bread?"

Saliva forms a pool in my mouth, almost causing me to drool. "Yes."

Mom turns her head and faces the waiter with a smile.

"Good choice, ladies." Erik hurries off to place the order.

Mom squeezes the honey packet into her tea, stirs the mixture with her spoon, and rests the utensil on the saucer. "I knew what you were going to say, Beth. I miss our times too. So how does once a week sound about having time together?" She points to me and then drags her finger to herself. "To shop or whatever?"

"Are you serious, Mom?"

"Absolutely. Just you and me."

"Mom, it would be terrific to have 'Mom and Me Time' back." I'm glad to see that she's improving on her vows.

"It's back. She reaches high over the table."

I slap her palm.

With the bread and salads now on the table, I reach for a slice of garlic bread, take a bite, and chew. Savoring the taste, I pray in my head. *Jesus, when am I supposed to bring up the Daddy issue?* Not receiving a prompt, I begin with what is still a dilemma: the test. "Mom, I want—no, I need—to tell you what I've been dealing with these past few weeks." She leans closer. "I've been totally bummed about the SAT. Susan and Jimmy will register, but I didn't want to follow just because."

"Honey, Robert and I want you to go to college. You've got the grades, and it's important to further your education."

"I understand it more now since I met with Mr. Max a few days ago, but I'm clueless about what I want to do with my life after next year. When I go to a college or university, I want to know why I'm there. I agreed to register after Max's encouragement, but now I'm seriously praying that Jesus will show me where I'm supposed to go and what He wants me to do after the college entrance exam." I rest my back against the cushion and breathe out a sigh.

Erik sets the meals down. "Ladies, is there anything else I can get for you?"

"No, Erik. Everything smells delicious. Thank you."

"Enjoy." He excuses himself and wheels around 180 degrees to serve the couple seated in the booth across from us.

"Mom, I'd like to pray." She closes her eyes and bows her head. "Thank You, Jesus, for time with Mom tonight. I am grateful for answers about Daddy. Thank You for the food. Amen." A moment of silence slides by. Then I dive into the most fabulous juicy red prime rib ever.

Contentment washes over Mom's face as her curls her lips surround a forkful of salmon. Dabbing the corners of her mouth with a napkin, she rests the fork on the plate. "If you want to talk when the scores come back, I'm here."

"I know. Thanks for listening."

I stir my Coke with the straw while I ponder the next topic. "Mom, I know it's a dead issue, but your now purplish-blue sweater is a colorful picture of what my life has been like with Molly these past weeks." Mom appears confused, so I fill her in. "I'm tired of her adolescent game of 'I'll be your friend today but don't know about tomorrow.' I've questioned her, but she refuses to publish the reasons behind her behavior." I stab a crouton and romaine lettuce with my fork. Chew and swallow hard. "I really tried to win the 800 meter race, but my head was all cluttered up with Molly stuff. It's a miracle I even qualified for the 3,200."

"Honey, I hear your pain. It's sad to hear this because you have been friends since you were little tykes. She might come around. I appreciate your perseverance to regain what you once had. However, there's someone in the family who needs your attention."

"I know what you're going to say, Mom. It's been hard to accept Robert because I miss Daddy so. Why did Daddy go away and never come home? Why didn't I get to say goodbye? For ten *long* years, I've been waiting for the answers. I tried to get you to talk and tell me everything on the tenth anniversary of Daddy's disappearance. Guess the timing was off." I gulp down the liquid in my throat and gawk at my hands that tightly twist the napkin. Then I stare into Mom's eyes, waiting. Then I sniffle back a tear.

Mom plucks Kleenex from her purse. "Okay, Beth. You have deserved to know the truth for years. I'm sorry for locking away the day that your father left. I didn't know handle my own pain, let alone my six-year-old's trauma. I didn't know what to do, so I suppressed the facts and fell in love with Robert. I knew he would be a good stepfather to you. I thought that was enough to go on with life." Mom takes minutes to wipe tears.

I reach for and hold her hand. Between tears, I say, "Mom, thank you for telling me. I see how hard this is for you. Please continue."

"Okay, Beth. Here's what happened that tragic day. It was a warm early spring morning. You bounded out the back door, anxious for the trip to the mountains. Your father teetered on the threshold, and his body fell on the asphalt. The sound of his bones meeting the ground rock was nasty, horrible. I screamed, 'Help.' Then while shaking like a leaf, I dialed 911.

"An ambulance rounded the corner. Lights flashed—red-orange, red-orange. It backed onto the driveway. Paramedics wheeled out a gurney, picked up John, laid him on the bed, and slammed the doors. The siren blared. The vehicle screeched down the street and melted slowly like an ice cube in the distance.

"You stood there, Beth, shedding endless tears and screaming, 'Daddy. Daddy.' I knew you wanted him to come back and give you one more kiss and say everything would be okay. I saw you rubbing the sockets of your eyes with your tiny fists, but the only thing I could do at the time was take you to Mrs. Feldman's house. She was our next door neighbor at the time.

"Then I rushed to the hospital to be with your father. Your daddy died from leukemia in the hospital days later. I didn't take you to the funeral because I thought you were too young." Mom lets out a very long breath. "It feels good to finally share the truth about that terrible day. Please, please, Beth, forgive me. I'm so sorry."

Mom lets go of my hand and sits back in her chair with the napkin over both eyes and weeps quietly.

"Mom, I forgive you," I say as I mop up my own tears. "Because I didn't know what happened to Daddy, I searched for him for years. One day, I thought I saw him working as a gardener across the street. When I rushed over and saw that the man wasn't even a look-alike, I stood in front of the man like a statute, frozen in time. Stunned because I wanted him to be Daddy." My breath comes in gulps now. "I ran and cried until my eyes couldn't stay open."

"Beth, you never told me about that. Why?"

"How could I? You never wanted to talk about Daddy so I figured it was pointless to tell you."

Mom and I sit in silence. After minutes, Mom composes herself and reaches for my hand, making no move to brush away her tears. In the candlelight, she's the most beautiful Mom in the world.

I squeeze her hand with both of mine. "I always suspected he died, but I just wanted an explanation. I needed you to tell me what happened and why. Yes, I forgive you."

As soon as I say the word "forgive," the blanket of pain and anxiety that has held me caged like a bird for ten years lifts. I'm finally content. Mom pulls back her hand to wipe her tears. "Would you like to go to the cemetery and visit the graves? Maybe then you'll be able to have the closure you need."

"Yes. Yes, but can I go alone."

"Think you should. It's time."

"What are the visiting hours?"

Mom rubs her chin. "Think Rose Hills Memorial Park & Mortuary opens at six."

"I'll be there when it opens, and it will give me plenty of time to say my goodbyes and be home for Jimmy at ten. On the way home tonight, can we stop at the store and get two bouquets of flowers?"

"Absolutely."

"Can we celebrate this dinner's conversation with dessert?"

"Yes." Mom flags Erik down. "Could we have an order of cherries jubilee?"

"Certainly. I'll be right back with the dessert and two spoons."

After the yummy meal, rewarding conversation, and fabulous dessert, Mom and I step outside and link arms. Temperature probably in the seventies with a light wind. Smells from nearby rosebushes—soft, fragrant. Excellent conditions to end an awesome day.

❋ ❋ ❋

The next morning, with a mission on my mind, it's easy to greet the day at five thirty. I dress quickly and fly down the stairs to the kitchen. I read the words on a sticky note stuck to the fridge. "Beth, hope you find peace at the cemetery."

When I open the fridge door, there's a brown bag with my name written on it. Inside the bag is my most favorite breakfast in ready-to-go containers. I think, *Thank You, Jesus, for giving me back my mom.* With breakfast in hand, I head for the car.

"Okay, God, it's just You and me." With Jesus as my passenger and the Kleenex box between us, I back out of the driveway. Getting past the stops and starts in city traffic, I round a curve. The words "Rose Hills" stand out in huge block white letters. My car inches like a turtle on the paved road. It gives me time to prepare my heart.

Mom's instructions echo through my mind: *Your daddy's marker is around the second corner and under a tree near the Japanese garden and lake.*

I stop the car and let it idle for a moment before I proceed. My heart pounds; my hands and face ooze beads of perspiration. I whisper under my breath, "Calm down." My eyes catch a family as they form a huddle, cry, and whisper. I shed tears of sympathy for their loss and my own. Parking off to the side, I walk over to Daddy. When I see the marker, I realize how much Mom loved him. It's shaded from heavy rains and the hot sun.

The marker reads,

John David Paine
1964–2002
Beloved Husband and Daddy.

I fall to my knees, place the bouquet of white orchids into the permanent vase, and weep. I whisper, "Daddy, I loved you. Miss you." I fold my legs underneath me. More tears rush down my cheeks. I squeeze my eyes shut and clearly recall the awful, horrible moment ten years ago. I see Daddy, trip, fall, and land on the asphalt. I kneel next to him, cry hard and scream. "Daddy, I love you so much." I throw myself on top of Daddy. "Don't leave me." The ambulance arrives. The scene fades.

Minutes later saltwater tears find their way to my mouth and bring me back to where I am now—in front of Daddy's grave marker. Even though the words are painful, I manage to say, "I know God had a reason for taking you from me. I will *never, ever* forget you."

With tears still falling, I bow my head and whisper a prayer. "Thank You, God, for Daddy and time for closure." As I lift my head and open my eyes, a very long breath escapes. "Daddy, I'm giving you orchids as a present from Mom. She said you gave her these flowers, one for every anniversary. We both loved you—always will."

A mother and daughter arrive at a close site. The words on the child's balloon: "World's Greatest Daddy." The little girl draws her fist to her eye and looks up at her mother.

I stand and throw Daddy a kiss. Then wipe a tear. "You *were* the greatest."

With the bouquet of pink rosebuds in hand, I side step the markers until I locate Bma's grave. It lies directly in front of the rose garden. *Mom's so thoughtful.* Under the name and years of life, I read, "Mother, Mother-in-law, and Grandma Bma."

"Thank you for being a perfect grandma. You saw my pain and took me to church. I will always remember you for that. My friend Jimmy told me that all believers get to spend eternity with Jesus. My deepest desire is see you again." Smiling, I lay my hand on the marker and pat it, then I inhale a hint of baby powder in the rosebuds and set them in the vase. I throw Daddy and Bma one last kiss and walk like a tortoise back to my car.

My Chevy Cruze creeps back toward the entrance of the cemetery. I turn right and head for home and life.

Chapter 19

When I open the back door, I see Mom pulling muffins from the oven. I rush to her side and plant a kiss on her cheek. "What did you make, Julia?"

She laughs. "Blueberry muffins. Want one?"

"Thanks for the nice bagel surprise breakfast this morning. I ate it, but for some reason, I'm still starving. I'll get the butter and start the tea water. Thanks for your suggestion about the cemetery."

"You're welcome. Do you feel better now?"

"Yes, I do. When I first arrived, my nerves were a mass of knots because I didn't know how I was going to deal with the reality. But after I threw each of them a kiss, an unexplained peace swept over me. I know I will have days when I miss Daddy, but I'm going to focus on the good days the three of us had." I reach for the butter in the fridge. "And I will always be grateful for Bma taking me to church."

Mom and I sit in comfortable silence while we each devour two muffins and sip herbal tea. After I swallow my last bite, I stand and rest my hand on her shoulder. "Since I have time before Jimmy arrives, I'm going to jump in the shower."

Minutes later, Mom knocks from the other side of my bath-room door and opens it just enough to give me privacy and hear her over the shower water. "Beth, Jimmy's here."

"Great! Thanks. I'll be down in a few."

She respectfully closes the door with a gentle click. With the swiftness of a cheetah, I dress in my Miss Me cropped denim jeans with bling on the pockets, sandals, and lavender T-shirt and sweep my hair into an updo. Then I stand in front of my open closet and chew on a nail as I think about dinner. In less than a millisecond, I drape the coral chiffon dress with cap sleeves over one arm, gather a pair of tan Toms wedges, and fly down the stairs to my date.

The car keys jingle below Jimmy's palm. "You look fab as always. Ready?"

"As soon as I get the lunch, for sure." The excitement of sharing the day with my hot boyfriend is over the top. If this kind of excitement were to be measured on the Richter magnitude scale, it would probably register 9.0 or higher. I brush past his blue Polo shirt and cargo shorts. My nostrils tingle at his fresh, clean scent. I hurriedly pop into the kitchen and add two Cokes to the cooler.

Mom slips into the kitchen and squeezes my shoulder with her hand. "Have a great day. Love you."

"Will. Love you too. Thanks for packing the lunch." I scurry back to Jimmy with the cooler in hand.

"Ready. Let's go." Jimmy takes the cooler. I open the front door. The warm sun greets us.

As I settle on the passenger seat, Jimmy fastens his seat belt, backs out of the driveway, changes gears, and presses the gas pedal. He performs all of these movements with caution. Grateful, I reach over and rub his arm.

"What's that for?"

"Just love our time together."

"Ditto."

Air from my open window fingers my hair. A strand falls and tickles my neck. I tuck it behind an ear, sit sideways, and face Jimmy's profile. "You'll never guess what I found in the suitcase when I came home from the cemetery this morning."

He takes his eyes off the road for a sec. "The cemetery? This morning?" Then he concentrates back on the traffic.

"Yes and yes. At dinner last night with Mom—" I stop myself. "Thanks for your prayers. Dinner was a success. Mom told me that Daddy died. Then with tears, she said he passed from leukemia. She apologized for not talking sooner. After dinner, she suggested I visit Daddy and Bma's graves. This morning I said goodbye to each of them."

"Must've been a God thing." Jimmy swallows. "I'm so proud of you."

"You have taught me so much about love and perseverance. You wanted to know about your dad, so you went after the answer because you were in pain. I have to confess that I didn't know how to share the pain of losing my grandma. That was the reason I couldn't talk that Sunday morning when I called and told you about her passing. I was in shock, so I stuffed it. That is, until I came home. I shared my pain with Mom and Dad and shed tears, telling my parents how much my grandma meant to me. Thank you, Beth, for teaching me to share." He reaches for my hand and squeezes it gently.

A heavy mist covers my eyes. "Thank you for sharing. Now I—we—have peace from what was driving us crazy."

"Yes." Jimmy taps the break. The car comes to a quiet stop at the red light. If only he knew how much his obedience to the driver's manual is appreciated. He turns his head to look my way. "So, Beth, back to the suitcase, what did you find?"

"A porcelain pig dressed in a yellow leotard and tutu. I cracked up when I first saw the animal. Then I was blown away because if I stood her on her hands, her toes pointed toward the heavens. If I stood her on her feet, her hands raised to God. My theory was that it had been put in the suitcase by mistake. But then, God reminded me that Stephanie loves ballet and her favorite color is yellow. It will be a present from me to her when I get home. I'm excited to see Steph's reaction."

Jimmy says, "You'll have to share what she says, Beth."

"Don't worry. I will because there's no secrets between us, right?"

"Right, Beth."

Jimmy enters the freeway. The cars in the slow lane move over, and give Jimmy space. He waves as they speed by. He sneaks a look from the road to me. "What were the other items you found, or is it a secret?"

"Not a secret. The first three items were a telephone, a note, and a postcard. At first, I didn't understand, but now—"

"I'm anxious to hear about the others and what you learned, but hold on." He parks in a space at the Santa Monica State Beach, jumps out, and opens my door. "It's such a nice day. Let's walk. You can finish the story if I don't throw you in the water."

"You wouldn't!"

"Wouldn't think of it." His grin is the length of a football field.

On the beach, we take off our sandals. I love the way the warm earth particles massage and hug my feet and love the smell of the wet salt air, the whine of the seagulls and the way the waves rise and fall, slow and evenly paced. Inches from the water's edge, I drop Jimmy's hand and sprint. My heart beats excitedly.

The wet sand coats the bottom of my feet like butter on bread. My strides—long and fast. My guffaws—loud. I jump over a clump of seaweed. Jimmy catches up and tags me. "You're fast."

Jimmy and I fall and lie on a dry patch of the gritty grains.

I watch clouds form wispy cotton balls, and float across the sky. Attempting to catch my breath, I throw my hand over my heart. "I want to qualify for the championship finals."

"Don't sweat it. Keep the faith. You'll get where God wants you."

Ideas where God might want me flash before my eyes faster than commercials. Jimmy nudges me in the ribs with his elbow. "You hungry for lunch?"

"Beyond description."

"I'll get the stuff from the trunk. Don't go away!"

"Jimmy, you're such a funny guy."

When he returns, we spread out the blanket and chow down on chicken, avocado, and red onion sandwiches on sourdough and sour cream and onion Doritos. I make a mental note to congratulate Mom for her awesome meal.

Jimmy reclines on the Hawaiian Islands beach blanket with his head propped up against the cooler. "Tell me about the next item."

I sit in my brother's favorite position, criss cross applesauce, and play with the sand. "Next was a stuffed bear with a crimson-striped appliqué in the form of a heart stitched over the center of his chest. I got a visual picture of the lashes Jesus took for me. I cried." I take a breath. "A red wooden apple followed the bear. Thanks to you"—I stop to throw Jimmy a grape.

When it's in the air, he barks like a seal and opens his mouth. He catches it in his hand. I suspect Jimmy's laughter is loud enough to reach an Eskimo in Alaska even though the person is three thousand miles away. I look around and see other people gawking and soften my giggles.

Able to hold down another giggle, I finish what I started to say. "I learned how sin entered man."

Jimmy sits up. "Wow. God was in the suitcase."

"Yep. It started with the letter," I say after I finish off the last of my drink. "Next was the calendar. For the longest time, I fished for the message. Then it was like I got struck with a lightning bolt when I saw the telephone, note, postcard, and calendar on my dresser. I caught on. My job now is to get priorities straight and work on relationships and watch what I say and how I say it."

"Know what you mean, Beth. I hate to tell you this because it's embarrassing, but my time with Jesus and family has slipped. I'm working on giving them quality time. Not just selfish minutes."

"It feels good to be open and honest with each other, doesn't it?"

Jimmy jumps up. "Yes, it does. You'll have to tell me about the other stuff later. Time to pack this stuff up and take a drive. I want to show you a place down the road. Might want to put on your sandals."

I quickly throw everything in the cooler, gather the blanket in an unrecognizable mass, and grab his hand.

After a quick drive, Jimmy opens the passenger door. My attention is drawn to musical tones. My heart pulses as I pull Jimmy toward the orange building. Just inside the door, I stop short. I let out a screech. "Never been on a carousel. It's the best surprise ever."

"I'm glad. Was pretty psyched when I saw it on the web. It's called the Looff Hippodrome." He reaches for his wallet. "It has been featured in a number of movies like the 1973 movie *The Sting*. Want to ride?"

Without answering, I head for a white horse.

Jimmy chooses a horse that resembles *The Black Stallion*. He goes up; I go down. I realize that jawing over the loud "June is Bustin' Out All Over" carousel music—fruitless.

I giggle so much that my sides ache. Jimmy dismounts and helps me down. "Thank you. Thank you."

"Beth, you're welcome. You're welcome. There's more."

"Another carousel?"

"No, a different place. But first, let's grab ice cream cones." He leads me to Soda Jerks a few steps away and across from the carousel.

I dump the idea of a cone and order the La Monica Ballroom sundae. Jimmy orders "The Sting" sundae. My ice cream treat is laced with hot fudge. Jimmy's has espresso and chocolate. I wonder how this day can get funner.

Jimmy and I stand next to the rail on the pier. I scoop a spoonful of pistachio nut ice cream into my mouth and watch the activity above and at sea level. Sea gulls dip into the ocean and soar with their catches. Children struggle with taut kite strings. A golden retriever barks and chases a red ball on the beach. I study Jimmy's eyes.

Jimmy, after a grin, says, "Ready for more animals at the Santa Monica Pier Aquarium?"

"Lead on."

My sandals *click, click, click, click* against my heels as I race down the wood steps with my date toward the blue and white building underneath the pier. Inside, Jimmy and I meander for hours around the various tanks. Inside the phylum discovery tank are my favorite blue, yellow, green, red, and striped jellyfish. I'm amazed at how God created and designed the umbrella-shaped bells and trailing lacelike tentacles. The scene blows me away. Before we find the door, I give him a quick kiss on the cheek. "The aquarium was great. This day has been awesome."

"It's not over, Beth."

"What's next?"

"Let's walk before we go to dinner. Want to hear more about the suitcase." Jimmy and I take off our sandals, walk in the water, and occasionally splash one another. "What was the next item?"

"Brain freeze. Where did I leave off?"

"The calendar."

"Um, after the calendar, I lifted a pink plastic rosebud. The penned words from the letter floated into my brain and reminded me to hold onto sweet memories. The rose, with the one you gave me, reminded me of the roses in Bma's garden. But when we weren't in the garden and I was bored, Bma would prop me up on her stool, and we'd make something I dreamed up and called Mush.

"Then on Monday, I pulled a pillow cover from the suitcase and read the embroidered words about marriage. I cracked up because we had just had a heated discussion in English Lit about Gatsby. In class, I blurted out how marriage is supposed to be forever." I stop to pick up a vacant and complete sand dollar. I pass it to Jimmy for him to study. "Do you want to get married?"

"Yeah, definitely. But when and who, only God knows."

"I want to get married too. But first, I need to get to know me so I'll be ready for the right life partner when he comes along."

A short intermission in conversation follows as Jimmy and I plop down on a dry patch of sand and copy a cluster of children as they dig and make a tunnel. I pull sand away from a spot. "The same day, I lifted a compact mirror and saw my reflection. Didn't understand until I heard another of Pastor Rosenburg's sermons. God showed me I was supposed to examine my heart. I remembered how ugly I have been toward Mom, Robert, and the kids.

"A handkerchief and a Bible with a wooden cross followed the mirror. I read the Bible verses and understand now that Jesus wants to teach me through his Word. I've discovered that the more time I spend reading the Bible, I love Jesus more.

"On Friday morning, the suitcase gave up a running shoe. Coach told me to run with perseverance. I thought the coach meant to run for the blue ribbons, but after accepting Christ, I understand it to mean that I need to follow Jesus and be an example for Him forever." I sneak a look at Jimmy from the corners of my eyes. "Think Jesus has the other shoe?"

He seems to catch the drift of my question. "No doubt about it. He's right here with you—us. Do you have any idea who left the suitcase?"

"Not really, but I have my suspicions about Coach Forsythe since he told me to run with perseverance. The same words were in the letter. Then Pastor Rosenburg… Maybe I should just be grateful for whoever left it. There's still a rattle in the suitcase. Think I'll open it tomorrow."

Jimmy lies down on his side and rests his head on a bent elbow.

I continue, "Understanding the reason for the suitcase and learning about the contents was frustrating. I have to admit that I really didn't understand God's love for me until I thought about each item and believed what they were supposed to mean to me. I know now that Jesus had a plan. Because He helped me, I was able to get the answers at the right time and in the right way. It's the best feeling ever to know and understand that God will never leave me and has something for me to learn each day."

"Jimmy nods, stands, and bushes off sand. "Let's get dressed for dinner."

The sun rests on the horizon. Gold diamonds bounce on the waves. Wood-scented smoke rises from fires on the beach and drifts in random directions. Suspect people will be chowing down on s'mores soon. Fun, but I love seafood more.

My boyfriend emerges from the restroom in his plaid short-sleeve button-up shirt, dark wash jeans, and gray Toms. He's such a mighty fine dude.

Our drive to Ocean Avenue Seafood Restaurant is short. The atmosphere inside the restaurant is casual but elegant. Warm autumn colors cover the floor, tables, and chairs. The hostess comes our way and shows us to a table on the patio. It overlooks the ocean and the pier.

Jimmy pulls out my chair and hurries around the table to sit. The talk between customers hushed, private. Soft music filters down from overhead speakers. Still able to still hear the pounding of the waves, the smell of salty air makes me hungrier than I ever been in my life.

"Hungry?"

I study the menu and keep my eyes on the prices. "Sure, but it's kinda spendy."

He rests his hand on mine. "Don't worry about it. This is our day." Jimmy's firm, quiet voice puts my mind at ease.

Moments later, the waitress places crab stuffed shrimp on the table under my nose and sets the wild Pacific swordfish in front of Jimmy. The conversation at dinner resembles a train out of control.

When Jimmy finishes his last bite, he rests his back against the high-back chair. "Think we could share the chocolate bread pudding?"

After the chocolate high this afternoon, I'm confident that I'll be up all night journaling. "More chocolate, sure."

Feeling just a tad overstuffed, I waddle next to my date on the way to his car. "A stuffed duck I am." I hear a soft chuckle next to me. When I'm settled on the passenger seat, I plant a peck on Jimmy's cheek. "Thanks for the day."

"Had a great day too."

"Wouldn't want it any other way." We jaw all the way home.

On the porch, he twirls me around and pulls me close. Our chins and lips meet. The kiss is soft and long. My foot leaves the pavement; my heart pounds. I'm light-headed. Jimmy releases me with another kiss on my cheek and whispers. "Let me know if you want me to pick you up for church."

"Will do. Thank you for a marvelous, fantastic day, Prince Charming."

Jimmy laughs, waves, and walks to the car. I suspect his lips are still touching his ears with a grin. I feel my lips doing the same. Trillions of stars dot the cloudless night. Got my wish: kiss under blinking diamonds. When the front door closes, I rest against the doorframe and hold onto the last moments of our day.

Chapter 20

Seconds later Stephanie's screams come from the living room and jar me from dreaming about my next date with Jimmy. "Ow. Mommy, it hurts."

I run. My sister sits on the couch. Huge tears fall over her lids and rush down her face. She pats her left yellow casted arm with her right hand. "What happened?"

Between tears Stephanie blurts out, "I fell at dance lessons."

I sit on the cushion next to Steph's head and brush her curls with my fingers. Mom stands next to me. "After a spin at ballet, Stephanie lost her balance and tumbled on her arm." Stephanie sniffles. "The doctor said she broke the ulna, the bone between the wrist and the elbow. The cast has to stay on for six weeks."

My sister wipes her face with her free limb. "It hurts. Can I have two more pills?"

"Sure." Seconds later Mom reappears with a glass of water and Ibuprofen.

Before I rush toward the stairs, I say, "Stephanie, I have a present. Hope it will cheer you up." I sprint up to my room, wrap the pig in tissue paper, and drop it in the gift bag that I bought on my way home from the cemetery. Then I dash back down to the patient.

Steph pulls out the porcelain figurine and giggles. "She's so cute!"

"Do you like it?"

Steph nods and holds the pig next to her heart. "Thank you, thank you. Where did you get it?" Mom sits, folds her hands in her lap, and leans forward.

"I got it from a very out-of-the-ordinary place. It reminds me of my ballet lessons. I hope the ballerina will cause you to remember your ballet lessons and days with Mom."

Across the room, I hear Mom sniffle. I take a deep breath, let it out slowly, and focus my attention to Mom. "Mom, what about church tomorrow?"

She concentrates on the injured one. "Stephanie, would you like to give Sunday school a try?"

"Yeah, after a good night's sleep."

"Great!" I stand, give my sister and Mom a hug, and hurry up the stairs to text Jimmy.

After a quick text, I change into my PJs and kneel beside the bed. "Dear God, Thank You for today. Please help Stephanie to heal fast. And please help this caffeine high to wear off soon. I need quiet strength for church tomorrow. Amen."

❋ ❋ ❋

When I pull into the church lot, Jimmy waves from the top step. He's snappy in his caramel-colored cargo pants, red Polo shirt, and sunglasses.

I watch Stephanie and RC escape from the confines of the car and run to greet Jimmy. They almost knock him over with bear hugs. Then my injured sister dances around in her bright yellow outfit and yellow cast as she waits for Mom and I to catch up.

I step from the driver's side and pause a moment to drink in the warmth of the sun on my face, my back, and my arms. The aroma of the flowers on the cherry trees floats through the air and finds its way to my nostrils—delicious. The chirps of the birds sound like one gigantic choir. I agree with their praises. Then I march with Mom to connect with Jimmy.

Jimmy reaches for my hand. Fearful that the pastor saw me run out Wednesday night, I pray under my breath. *God, please don't let him ask questions. Don't want to rehash my probs in front of the world.* My nerves shake and splinter.

Pastor Rosenburg reaches for my brother's hand. "What's your name, young man?"

RC wraps his short five-year-old fingers around the pastor's hand and stands tall. "My name's RC. It means Robert Cade."

A lady from a group walks over to Mom. "You have a nice, mannered young man."

Guess RC was listening because he produces what looks like the face of Mickey Mouse, so genuinely pleased with himself, and his cheeks grow into polished red beets. He responds bashfully, "Thanks."

When his cheeks return to a pale pink, I introduce Mom and Stephanie. Pastor Rosenburg extends his hand. "Nice to meet you both. I'm glad you could join us today." He faces my way. "It's great to have you back, Beth."

I blow out air. "Thanks." With my nerves in their rightful places, I almost feel comfortable enough to ask the pastor if he was the one who put the suitcase under the park bench but nix the idea.

Susan, Brian, and Josh rush from the back of the room. They join our group now in the middle of the commons, the place to gather and sip coffee. Matthew and the gang round a corner and lift their hands. Everyone, my brother and sister included, gives each a high five. The kids' smiles—large.

The now-large party disbands and fills two rows in the sanctuary. I sit between Jimmy and Mom. Carol leans over the back of my pew. "Beth, you were supposed to call me. What happened after Wednesday night? Been worried about you, girl."

I glance and curl my hand halfway around my mouth and whisper. "Tell you later. I'm good."

Jimmy nods and says to Carol, "Beth's more than good." A wink follows. He points to the choir as they march in.

Other voices fade as the choir fills the bleachers behind the podium. Mr. Holland motions for the congregation to stand and sing the words on the screen. After the last chorus of the third song, Pastor Rosenburg leans against and over the pulpit. "Before I start today's sermon, all kids from kindergarten through fifth grade are dismissed at this time to go to Sunday school."

Children's feet scramble. Babies whimper. Coughs erupt. The pastor sips water from a Styrofoam cup. The commotion dies down. "Okay, people, let's sing 'Rock of Ages.' He steps aside to let the music minister lead the congregation. My favorite song. Now I understand. God is my immovable Rock.

Mom faces my brother and sister and asks loud enough for me to hear. "Stephanie and RC, do you want to go to children's church?" The kids jump from the seats. Mom nudges me. "I'll be right back."

When the last notes of the chorus are sung, Mr. Holland motions for everyone to sit. Mom inches her way back in. "How are the kids?"

"Stephanie was a little fearful because of her arm, but she found a friend who's in her class at school. It didn't a take a minute before RC found Legos."

Now with Bible in hand, Pastor Rosenburg slips behind the pulpit and clears his throat. "For tonight's sermon, 'Courage to Follow,' we will learn about Joshua's courage. Please turn to the Book of Joshua."

I sit on the edge of my seat with my Bible open and learn so much about how to not fear and get the courage to press on with God's strength. Then after the benediction, I along with the rest of the youth group gather in the foyer. Carol dashes over and stands beside me.

"Carol, I'm sorry I didn't text you. Gave my pain and problems to Jesus when Jimmy and I went to the park Thursday afternoon. I accepted Jesus as Lord and Savior."

"Fabulous." I understand her hug to be genuine. She drops her arms. "Welcome to the FOB" (family of believers).

"Thanks."

Jimmy chases away quiet moments. "Think we should all go out for burgers, come back, and get into a mean game of volleyball. I have the key to the gymnasium." He holds the key up, proud of his show-and-tell time.

I bow out. "Not today. I drove Mom and the kids."

Mom spins halfway around. "Beth, take us home and then you and your friends can have a good time."

"Are you sure?"

Jimmy cups his hand around my shoulder and catches Mom's attention with his eyes.

"Mrs. Cade, please join us." The boy knows how to make points.

All lips spread into smiles; heads resemble those on Bobbing Head dolls.

RC and Stephanie beg, "Please?"

My mother places an arm around each child. "We'd love to join you." She takes a breath. "Beth, ride with Jimmy. I'll take good care of your car."

"Not worried. Thanks."

Jimmy rotates around. "Susan and Josh, are you up for an afternoon of fun? Heard the girls beat the guys in the last game. So—"

Susan interrupts with a sparkle in her eye. "The girls will be the winners again, if I play." I catch her tease but like her attitude.

"Josh says, "I'm in."

Everyone heads to cars. It's almost a pretty picture because Molly and Robert aren't here. I sigh. Maybe another day.

❋ ❋ ❋

After lunch, I, with all the other bodies, stand outside and wait for Jimmy to unlock the gym doors. The sun—red-hot. Glad I put on the SPF 30 ultra-protection sunscreen today. Jimmy says. "Let's agree to make it a three-game day because we have homework demands and school tomorrow."

Someone in the back yells, "We agree. Let's get out of the heat."

The doors fly open. Each team forms a circle around their captains. Like bees around the nest, excitement builds. Jimmy and Carol shout in unison, "Prepare for war," as they leave their groups and play the usual game of rock paper scissors. Jimmy wins.

Baritone laughter bounces off of the four walls. Feet pound like horses on the race track as players run to chosen spots on the court. Jimmy jumps and strikes the ball. It sails over the net with the power of a missile. The first game ends with a score in favor of the guys: twenty-five to twenty.

Next, Josh moves into the right back position. He rolls his fingers into a fist. The ball flies just above heads and dives toward the net. The net snatches its prey. James puts it back into play and passes it under the net to Sarah. She stands outside the white line and watches it soar high over heads. Another point for girls. Score: two to zip. *My suspicion: the girls' adrenaline flows as fast as mine.*

Celebrations continue to the end. Girls win the second game with a score of twenty five to fifteen. Matthew shouts, "Okay, team, step it up." The guys reach toward the roof in preparation for my hit.

My attack—mighty. It sails over the net. Volleys continue for at least five minutes. Girls' spirits continue to soar when continuous points multiply to the double digits for Carol's side.

The score changes for the worst: twenty four to twenty three in favor of the guys. Jimmy slams the ball. I scream, "It's mine!"

"No, I've got it," Carol shouts enthusiastically. She and I both reach for it. It bounces on the floor just beyond fingertips. Carol and I roll on the floor and laugh—weird but fun.

The guys shout in unison. "Kill. We win."

I stand and slap my hands against hips and march to an out-of-bounds area. "The girls demand a rematch Wednesday night." I should've given the spot to Carol. Couldn't control myself. Love this game and the group.

Jimmy consults the guys. "Okay, girls, you've got yourself a deal."

Both teams form the usual congratulatory lines. The group hangs and then leaves one at a time. Then Jimmy and I stand alone in the middle of the court. The ball rolls around on the floor. It's a perfect time to fill him in on the latest. "Gotta tell you what Susan wrote in her e-mail last night."

"Got my full attention." Jimmy sits on the ball.

"Susan typed, 'Todd revealed that he was smoking in the room where they keep the sheet music. It's known all over campus as the best place to light up because it's quiet and dark. He thought the match was out when he flicked it. On Monday, he's going to report to the front office and confess.'

"I wrote back. 'Sorry for him and your loss.'

"Got a quick reply from her. 'Don't think twice about it because he's KOJC (King of the Jerks' Club). Be good for him to dress in jail clothes for a while.'

"She ended the electronic message with a 'happy face' and 'Time to move on.'"

Jimmy stands. The ball rolls away. "Wow. I would have never guessed." He switches off the lights and closes the door. He and I walk hand in hand toward his car in silence.

"Me either because I suspected Greg because I saw cigarettes in his car. I stand next to the passenger door and give Jimmy a peck on the cheek. "Thanks for today. Mom and kids appreciated the lunch invite. The weekend has been *fabulous*."

Jimmy reaches for my chin. His soft lips and strong arms tempt me to stay forever in his embrace. A breeze comes between us. Jimmy releases his squeeze. "Want to go for ice cream?"

"Sounds yummy, but I've got homework and want to know what's in the suitcase. How about after practice tomorrow?"

"Home it is. Tomorrow, you can tell me what you found."

Chapter 21

I step into the hallway between the kitchen and the stairs. No sounds of any kind bounce off the walls. Must be Sunday afternoon nap time. I tiptoe up to my room, shut the door, sit pretzel-style on the floor, and pull the suitcase out from its comfortable spot. Then I rest my hands on the latches for what I believe to be the last time and take a deep breath.

The phone rings. I jump up and retrieve my cell from the backpack. "Hi, Molly." I faint hello and a sniffle follow. "Are you okay?"

"No," follows another sniffle.

"What's going on? How's Greg?"

"He has a ton of doctor's appointments plus physical therapy. His parents are on their way."

"Good. I'll pray for him a little more than I have been."

"Thanks. Can you tell me about your secret now and why church is so important to you?"

In shock at the turnaround, I say, "Well, I found a letter on the front of a suitcase. It talked about God stuff. I didn't understand, so I went to Jimmy and hoped he would explain the note, but it wasn't until I turned a mirror—one of the contents—around in my hand. After struggling, I looked at myself from the inside out. I know what it means to be a follower of Jesus now. I'm dying to tell you more about what I've learned, if you're willing to listen."

Another sniffle. "Maybe."

Hopeful, I breathe out a puff. "Could we have a real date to go shopping at the Galleria to talk about Jesus and my faith? I still don't know what to do with my life. But I'm taking one day at a time and counting on Jesus to grow me up. I don't feel alone anymore."

A deafening silence fills the lines. I take the moment of silence to pull a piece of notebook paper from my backpack; write "Prayer List" at the top; then jot down Molly's, Greg's, and Todd's names off

165

to the side. Then I realize God performed a U-turn in me. Before Jesus, I carried pain and walked with fear and hate. Now with Jesus, I'm a new me. I take advantage of a quiet moment and pray silently. *God, You blow me away. You changed me. I know You can change Molly, Greg, and Todd. I pray they will come to You and seek forgiveness for their sins. Amen.*

After my quick prayer, I switch the subject back to Greg. "Molly, when did you go to the hospital last?"

"Just got back."

"When will you visit next?"

"Dunno."

"Do you think we could go together soon?"

"Have to think about it. Gotta go." A click follows.

I start to bite off a nail and realize that changes don't come easy. Instead of tearing the nail off with my teeth, I run to the bathroom drawer for a fingernail file.

With my attention back on the suitcase, I unsnap the latches and open the lid all the way. A small notebook stands alone. It has a postage stamp from somewhere in Paris. Butterflies, in various colors, dot the cover. I flip the pages and find them blank.

On the blank pages, I read aloud as I write, "Dear Friend, I'm glad you picked up the suitcase. It was meant just for you. If you don't believe it now, you will understand it better after you examine the contents. It took me weeks to understand the significance of each item and how they related to my life. Take your time. Don't let fear, anger, pain, and hatred swallow you up. Embrace love."

I pause, chew on the end of my pen, and ask the person to do what I am about to do. "When you understand, put the items back in the suitcase, add a treasure of your own, and return the suitcase where you found it with a note. God bless. I'll be praying for you."

A tear slides down my cheek and drops on my hand. I grab a Kleenex, crawl over to my closet, pull out my jewel box, and separate collected knickknacks. A silver key chain with a heart attached catches my attention. "Perfect." I pray, "Lord, it is my prayer that the person who picks up the suitcase will make a decision to accept Jesus Christ as Lord and Savior. Amen."

Memories flood my mind as I add the key and replace each item but minus the ballerina. When the latches snap, I find myself feeling sad—sad that I have to part with it. But then, I'm grateful for the memory and what I learned. Then with one hand on the handle of the suitcase and the other wrapped around the notebook, I run down the stairs.

In the kitchen, I write a legible note and remember to add the date and time. "Mom, I went to the park alone. Be back in about an hour. If I'm delayed, I'll call. Love you, Beth." I leave it on the counter, check to make sure it's away from wind gusts and water, and dash toward the front door.

With the suitcase as my passenger, I drive back to Griffith Park. The trip is bittersweet because all types of goodbyes are hard for me. I step out from the driver's side and saunter over to my park bench. Gold shadows splash on the flowers and trees. A breeze ruffles the pages on the notebook.

A lump forms in the back of my throat as I bow my head. "God, this trip with the suitcase has been awesome. Thank You, Lord, for showing me what I needed to do to change. As I say goodbye to the suitcase, I pray that the finder will come to understand that You created, love them, and have a plan."

After my prayer, I lean over, slide the suitcase under the bench, release my grip, and place the notebook on top and walk away.

Someone calls, "Beth. Beth."

"Over here."

Robert comes around the corner. "Your mother told me you were in the park. Will you accept my invite to dinner?" Tears form in the corner of his eyes. "I care about you. I believe we need to spend some time together. What do you think?" He spreads his arms wide.

Tears cascade down my cheeks. "Yes, Dad, I'd love to go to dinner." His hug is different but good. I enjoy the moment. I look up and our eyes meet. "Got a question."

"I'll try to answer. What is it?"

"The kids in the youth group have a chance to volunteer at the Special Olympics this summer. If I decide to go to college, I can put it on the application. It will show that I completed three days of community service and learned how to love others. Could I join them?"

Robert smiles broadly and winks. "I'll have to think about it. But first, you have to tell me what you've been up to."

"Deal."

Hand in hand, my dad and I walk out of the park.

Discussion Questions

1. Have you had people disappear from your life? If so, describe how you felt.
2. Did you feel the tension between Beth and her mom?
3. What did you think about Molly? Did you hate her or feel sympathetic toward her?
4. Can you recall a time when you've been too preoccupied to listen to or care about someone? How do you think the other person felt when he or she saw that you didn't care?
5. Did you appreciate Jimmy and Beth's relationship? Why?
6. If you picked up the suitcase, how would you have interpreted the letter? Would you be interested?
7. Have you had people like Jimmy, Mr. Max, and Coach Forsythe encourage you? If so, in what ways?
8. Have you had a Greg in your life? Did you stop the relationship before a disaster occurred? What would be your advice to another young adult who finds themselves in a precarious relationship?
9. What about the character of Beth? Did you see her maturing?
10. Is communication hard for you? Do you see the benefits of talking and listening?
11. Do you believe we should strive to overcome our pasts?
12. How does forgiveness play a role in the story?
13. What themes from this story stood out to you? Do you know why those particular ones resonated with you?
14. If you were going to write an epilogue for *The Suitcase*, what future would you envision for Jimmy, Beth, and Molly?

About the Author

Priscilla Tate Gilmore's articles, stories, and devotionals for teens and adults have appeared in *The Christian Journal*, *Now What*, *Purpose*, *Live*, *Significant Living*, *Breathe Again*, *Pathways*, and *Take Five Plus*. *The Suitcase* is her first novel. She lives in Salem, Oregon, and has two grown children.

To God Be the Glory

CPSIA information can be obtained
at www.ICGtesting.com
Printed in the USA
BVHW042325021122
651026BV00001B/70